Advance Praise

"*The 4 Secrets of the Universe* is an absolute treasure! Paul unravels the biggest mysteries—time, space, and how everything connects—in such a clear and exciting way...it feels like a fascinating conversation with a brilliant friend who's constantly blowing your mind. If you're even a little curious about life's mysteries, or just love a book that makes you see things differently, you'll absolutely love this one! Highly recommended!"
—Maria MacDonald

"[*The 4 Secrets of the Universe*] ...it's even better than *The Book of Manifesting* (which I loved—and rarely for me, have read it 3 times). It's essential reading."
—Llewellyn author, Richard Webster

"*The 4 Secrets of the Universe* is one of the most powerful books I have read... It is packed with questions I would have never thought to ask but very grateful to know the answers for. It is opening my heart... and shifting my consciousness."
—Aylin Kotapish

"Congratulations—you channel the highest vibration there is. You come closer than anyone in describing God."
—Spirit channel, William Perry

Other Works by This Author

The Book of Manifesting

Mysteries, Prophecies, and the Hollow Earth

*Poems of Life, Love,
and the Meaning of Meaning*

Poet Gone Wild

Sojourn

The Lightness of Being

All About the Soul's Journey

Infinite Healing Trilogy

*Poems and Messages for the
Loss of a Loved One*

*Poems and Messages for the
Loss of Your Animal Companion*

Healed in Timelessness

The 4 Secrets
of the
Universe

Making the 'You' in Universe

PAUL GORMAN

Copyright © 2024 Paul J. Gorman
All Rights Reserved

 Year of the Book
135 Glen Avenue
Glen Rock, PA 17327

ISBN 13: 978-1-64649-436-1 (print)
ISBN 13: 978-1-64649-437-8 (ebook)

Cover photo by author, Western Maryland
Interior images licensed by Depositphotos.com, Shutterstock.com, and iStockphoto.com unless otherwise noted.

No part of this publication may be reproduced, distributed, or transmitted in any form or by any means, including photocopying, recording, or other electronic or mechanical methods, without the prior written permission of the author, except in the case of brief quotations embodied in critical reviews and certain other noncommercial uses permitted by copyright law.

Library of Congress Control Number: 2024921646

Disclaimer:
This book contains spiritual messages and information, recommendations, and insights. It does not contain financial or medical advice. Seek medical attention when necessary from a knowledgeable health professional.

Future trends mentioned are a current snapshot that is changing, and will vary for each individual in every moment.

I do not favor one particular religion, country, or political party—just peace and well-being for all people, and all of life.

Contents

Foreword 1
Introduction 2
Five Main Lessons 6
  C+ 9
Rejuvenation 11
Diet and Nutrition 14
Detox Soup 18
Laying on the Left Side 21
Stonehenge 22
Only One Variable 26
  The Joke Is On Me 27
The Most Powerful Manifesting Engine 30
Programming of a Loving Intention 33
Illumination of Your Desires 35
Healed in God Mind Instantly 38
The Earth Merkabah 40
God Mind Recognition of Itself 43
As Healed as a Person Can Get 46
An Alkaline Body 49
Activation of a Mental Pain 53
  Now They Are Light 53
An Energetic Adjustment 56
An Investment Has 8 Characteristics 59
An Alien Entity 61
A Conundrum of Love and Non-love 62
Only One Antidote 65
The Devil Entity 70
A Non-love Repellant 74

Please Allow Me to Introduce Myself 76
The Titanic 80
On the Agenda..82
IHS 85
A Giant, Entertaining Hate Festival 87
The Earth's Loving Protection Grid....................90
Another Human Era 92
  My Moment With You.. 94
Disabled Beyond Repair 97
Laser Platforms..101
Intrusions into the Inner Earth 103
The North Pole Is Shifting Rapidly................... 106
The 5 Stages of Death.. 108
A Person's Spirit...111
A Guardian Angel... 113
A Lifetime Ending 115
Lifetime Agreements..123
A Godependent Relationship............................126
  A Bull Recalls His Time in a China Shop 127
Angels and Guides...129
Life Preview...132
Other Lifetimes 134
Soul Mates...138
A Past Life 140
  My Past Life Memory 142
An Instance of Distance 143
A Body Designed for 2.......................................145
A Courier of Important Messages.....................148
A Loving Ideal 150
Ascended Master Light Energy......................... 155
A Light That Has No Properties........................ 157

Allowing All That Is Non-existent 160
Dreamscaping 163
Godscape 166
An Impossible Dream 167
Dream Life 170
God Mind Has No Center 172
Love Is Me 175
   Love Is Me 177
Secret of the Universe #1 181
   Heart of Godness 184
All Devil's Day 188
Demon Perspective 190
Repairing the Earth's Grid 194
Secret of the Universe #2 196
Secret of the Universe #3 198
   Always One in My Eyes 201
A Healing Anecdote 204
   100% 207
Secret of the Universe #4 209
The 4 Secrets 212
   You'll Love When You See 213
Allowing Abundance 217
Setforward 219
   You'll See Only Me 220
Déjà vu 224
All There Is and Is Not 228
   All But Me 230
To Hell in a Handbasket 232
A Bigger Problem 234
The Key 237
Earth Spirit 238

Reality in My Favor 240
   Pleasant Surprises 242
Animal Dreams 244
The Fairy Kingdom 246
A Game of Love 249
   You Will Not Be Alone 251
A-B-C Land 253
   Always With Me 255
Andromeda 256
Field of Dreams 260
A Deal to Heal 262
   Something I Bring 264
Life's Active Projector 265
My Cup Runneth Over 269
A Learning Lesson 271
Akashic Records 272
God Mind in God Mind 275
A Separation Is Not Possible 277
Flow-ers of Light 279
Invited by the Earth 283
A Loving Vibration 286
God Mind's Home on the Earth 289
Airborne Acids 291
Update from the Inner-Earth 293
Of Biblical Proportions 295
Convenient for You to Heal In 297
Good Answer 300
Mandolin Dreams 305
A Musical Vibration 307
Message from My Brother 310
Take Another Red Pill 315

Only As We 319
   Only As We 320
A Demon Can Alter Itself 323
The Innermost Point of God Mind 326
My Universal Projection 328
   I'll Love Being You 329
Why Not? 330
Affirmations 331
Afterword 338
Glossary 339
About the Author 341

"An answer to every question is within the grasp of every soul. For he that seeks shall find, and they that knock, to them it shall be opened."

—*Edgar Cayce*

Foreword

The 4 Secrets of the Universe was written immediately following the publication of *The Book of Manifesting*, in the spring of 2024. It is helpful but not necessary to have first read *The Book of Manifesting*, which explains how we create our realities, and the nature of God itself.

This book continues with topics that were introduced there and in my other books to explore them further—much further—as far as I could go.

What if you could ask God anything? What if it was impossible not to get an answer?

It is only possible to not allow an answer.

Prepare to journey through consciousness—life and death, past and future—from the inner-earth to a nearby galaxy, all the way to the outer edge of the universe, ultimately arriving back at the beginning—the center of your being.

> "The longest journey is the journey inward."
>
> —Irish Proverb

Introduction

This is a book of my questions to God—with God's answers. The conversations are profound with new and important insights.

Some of my questions are practical, and the answers are always interesting and informative.

What is God? It says, *"I am all that we can be, as an infinite light from all that you can be."*

My dialogue with God, or God Mind, is often humorous, highlighting the spiritual concepts. This book also contains astounding messages from other energies and entities—and I won't spoil the surprises by revealing their identities in advance.

The 4 Secrets of the Universe continues the themes from my previous books, which are:

1. Life is a dream that is temporary, and like most dreams, it seems very real.
2. We are dreaming that we are apart from God, not a part of God.
3. The universe is a hologram of light—the electromagnetic spectrum.
4. Light has speed, requiring distance—or time and space.
5. The purpose of the dream is to heal our minds by motioning back to God.

6. Only love in each moment is real, which is God.
7. Non-love in the dream is not a part of God, and is therefore an illusion in the dream.
8. Illusions of non-love are allowed in the dream—allowed to heal.
9. Suffering is only in my mind—buying into the illusion.
10. Healing and peace can only be in my mind.
11. A healed mind has peaceful, loving thoughts—aligning in Oneness with God.
12. A healed mind loves life and loves itself.
13. Nature and animals are healed in the Mind of God. Nothing in nature hates life, or itself.
14. Our minds create the interactive dreams of our lifetimes as illuminating projections.
15. Before incarnating, we choose our lifetime challenges to heal in them.
16. We heal our minds by halting non-loving thoughts about ourselves and others.
17. A healed mind allows God Mind and manifests its desires.
18. Allowing God Mind heals the mind instantly, and the body in time.
19. Death is the end of the dream, waking us up in our home—Oneness with God.
20. The mind and spirit do not die, only the temporary body dies.

21. Death is a decision made on the mental and spiritual levels, and can be reversed, even moments after death.
22. You do take it with you—the love and creativity in our lives are entrained into our souls.
23. I am awake in the dream, aware of the illusion that is healing.
24. I am an eternal aspect of God, allowing all that is not God to heal in love—which is all there is.
25. God is expressed as kind and loving thoughts, which only exist in the present moment.
26. Love heals the mind, and perpetuates the illumination of God in eternity.

I can't say that I have a healed mind, but I'm learning—and healing. My messages say that life is a hard school, because it allows us to learn the hard way by experiencing mental and physical pain.

Now I know the answer to every test—which is to choose a loving thought. If I know the answer to every test, I will no longer be tested. Now that's a school I can enjoy.

The life-school has a curriculum of activities that are a continuous feedback loop of loving, living, and learning—on the planet of love and non-love.

My goal is to opt-out of the lessons on non-love, or at least not repeat them. They are the difficult lessons where self-punishment is the penalty for failing a test.

The tests literally never end until you pass. You cannot graduate until you learn, though you will understand when your time in the life-school ends.

You will then prepare and choose the next life-school challenge that you want to experience and learn from.

This can be the workbook that will help you to skip ahead—advancing in the school of consciousness while only taking the enjoyable classes in which you choose to advance yourself.

"Love" is our education—taught in every moment—and starts with loving ourselves. Love is God, or all there is—illuminating in our kind and loving thoughts.

Kind and loving thoughts are an expression of God and will allow our desires to manifest. Our minds heal the moment we realize that God or Oneness cannot be two, except in a dream, and it can only be love.

Note: The 'life-mind' is the logical and linear left-brain hemisphere, which heals into the 'Light Mind', the abstract and intuitive right-brain hemisphere—which opens in God Mind.

The term 'God Mind' is interchangeable with 'God', 'Mind of God', 'love', and 'Oneness'—and 'God Mind' is used mostly going forward.

Let's begin. [Imagine a very loud and annoying school bell.]

You arrived at the perfect time.

Five Main Lessons

I understand that from a soul's perspective, the Earth is a hard school, so strong souls come here.
A hard school means allowing students to learn the hard way.
All schools have harder and harder courses, and you progress through them—allowing each student to learn and elevate himself or herself to the next higher level.
Higher levels require more work—all as homework in life's lessons.

Is the Earth for stronger souls, or does it produce stronger souls?
It allows illumination for healing, advancing souls' awareness in higher consciousness.
All move higher in life, or in losing their lives—so all advance as they move higher in their illumination in God Mind.
All aligning with God Mind are indestructible, meaning infinitely strong.

Are souls that are not aligning with God Mind destructible?
All not aligning with God Mind is illusory, meaning not in a form to be destroyed.

You mentioned "*homework in life's lessons.*" Are there an infinite number of lessons to learn?
Illumination is infinite; the number of lessons is finite.

How many lessons are there?
Only 5 main lessons, with many variables and variations.

What are the 5 main lessons that we need to learn on Earth?
1. *Allowing is loving. All you do not allow is not loving, making it an illusion not in God Mind.*

2. *Loving life means loving yourself. All thoughts flowing from God Mind are loving and generous; all not loving and generous are not from God Mind and illegitimate—halting loving life or yourself.*

3. *All heals in time, or in no time—meaning in losing one's life. Healing in time means loving life and yourself, or #2. All heals in allowing it, or #1.*

4. *A healed mind can manifest its desires—only if they are healed in God Mind as loving thoughts, or #2.*

5. *All thoughts that are loving heal the life-mind in God Mind—allowing it, loving it, and manifesting it—or numbers 1-4.*

The common denominator is having "*loving thoughts.*"
All flow from God Mind in your mind allowing illumination of it—making God Mind healed thoughts that manifest your desires.

What's not to love about that? I guess that's the test.
All schools have testing to measure performance. You can get an 'A' for improvement, or an effort illuminating God Mind in your mind.
Effortless illumination means you graduated in life on Earth, meaning the next higher grade is in another dimension.

Which Dimension?
The 5th Dimension is higher—the 4th is for life-minds that are still healing.

C+

This poem and others in this book, unless noted otherwise, are from my book *The Lightness of Being*, healing conversations with God Mind, written in rhyming verse. The poems start with a thought, a feeling, or a question from me, and the responses from God Mind are in italics.

C+

You would think
  I'm not afraid to fail
I've had enough practice
  left a steady trail

of poor judgment
  missteps and errors
regrettable mistakes
  now memorable terrors

Think of life
  as learning classes
where grades are for improvement
  and your effort passes

much more than that
  your score would reach
to the higher range
  so you could teach

that the lesson is
  the lesson you earn
from each experience
  you had to learn

*a better thought
  to know and discern
what can't be taught
  so each gets their turn*

*to learn from mistakes
  and repeat them no more
to take a life course
  and get a good score*

*you are given chances
  to retake each test
move on to the next
  and forgive the rest*

*that is the way
  to be a success
and in the end you can say
  I did my best*

*(you will also be judged
  on the effort you made
but will be grading yourself
  on Graduation Day)*

*[I see you just gave
  yourself a grade
the course isn't over
  there's still time for an 'A'*

*and I'll give you hints
  tell you what to say
love is the answer
  the rest of the way]*

Rejuvenation

You had once said that I could rejuvenate myself up to 30 years. How can I do that?
All rejuvenation illogically halts an illogical belief in your progressing in illusory timelines, meaning illogical mindsets that are not healing—nor are they helpful.

How can I halt the illogical belief in time?
Allow each moment in life to be the only moment in your life.

Will I stop aging?
All aging illuminates in the belief in decay.
God allows you to believe in illogical thinking, meaning illogical thoughts of having enough time.
Heal your mind by affirming this, "My life is a light in the Mind of God, illuminating eternally."
Halt decay by believing in God Mind's infinite illumination in yourself.

Okay—is there something I could visualize?
Imagine God Mind illumination holding open your DNA, illuminating in God Mind and in your mind, healing each strand—including invisible ones.
Life heals in beliefs, so believe the light is repairing and rejuvenating each cell, membrane, organ, and function in the body.

Allow cells to heal in loving them, and hydrating them with healing water that has been structured in a bamboo and river stone flowform.[1]

What else?
Allow natural sounds of birds and water flowing their illuminating power to heal your mind.
Nothing heals in darkness—meaning only positive, loving thoughts heal the mind's illusion of darkness.
Allow the healing illumination in plants and animals to sustain your diet—only animals in small quantities.
Allow healing light rays from the sun to illuminate your skin, activating its mechanisms for healing the body.
Allow the mind to meditate on the infinite illumination of all of them.

Would I stop aging, or could I rejuvenate 30 years younger?
All cells that are renewing themselves will illuminate in a more youthful state, meaning in a younger, healed illumination.

More than 30 years younger?
"30" means healing on an illogical timeline, and healing means ideal—so 30 years or more is an imaginary timeline to illuminate in.

---

[1] Explained on page 46.

"A butterfly counts not months but moments, and has time enough."

—*Rabindranath Tagore*

Diet and Nutrition

I eat some chicken, and occasionally some beef and salmon because they are sustainable—but would not want to personally kill the animals. Should I be buying the meat—basically paying someone else to kill them?

All animals have a loving connection to God Mind, meaning all animals have healed minds that do not suffer.

All animals halt non-loving thoughts, and allow God Mind a home in their minds.

Do we need to eat animal proteins and fats, or is vegetarianism a healthier diet?

A diet of all plant fiber allows cells to become light energy converters, activating God Mind light in your DNA.

Won't that happen anyway, even if we eat meat?

Animal fats and proteins inhibit the conversion of light into energy in the bodies of humans.

Whoa!

A diet devoid of plants and grains has about 8 or 9 percent of the energy conversion that a body needs to function optimally.

A diet of all plants and grains has 100 percent of its energy converted into heat and light that cells, organs, and glands are designed to heal, grow, and function from.

Is it harmful to eat a small percentage of animal protein during the day?
It can be harmful if the animals have been injected with antibiotics and animal vaccines that will be ingested with the meat.

What if it is organic?
About 18-19 percent of energy is lost in digestion, making all animal fats and protein an energetic drain on the body.

Wouldn't we have a deficiency in nutrients or some vitamins if we did not eat some beef, chicken, or fish?
All are bioavailable in fruits, nuts, seeds, grains, and greens.

What would you recommend for me as a prototypical meal?
A grain and green salad with fermented vegetables on it, plus a soup made from any kind of plant and root vegetable that is edible.

I like it—but didn't see any pizza or tacos on the menu :)
Both of them can be healthy if the ingredients are healthy.

I just read that vegetarians can be deficient in vitamins B-12 and D, Omega 3 fatty acids, calcium, iron, and zinc.
All of them can be found in vegetarian sources.

Is it good to 'eat with the season'—fruits and greens in the summer, and root vegetables in the winter?
A good diet has each season in a 15-week rotation.

What do you mean?
For about 4 months, eat all greens and not legumes or grains; then for about 4 months eat all greens, legumes, and grains—meaning alternate grains and legumes in every other 4 month period of rotation.

Where do eggplant, mushrooms, avocados, and potatoes fall in that diet?
All are beneficial in both of the periods mentioned.

So, it is really an 'elimination diet'—eliminating peanuts, beans, lentils, chickpeas, hummus, etc. out of the diet for 4 month intervals.
Allowing digestion of legumes to rest, while enzymes do other healing work in the body.

What about eggs, cheese, and yogurt?
Eggs have an enzyme for healing the brain's protective barrier. Cheese has enzymes that ferment in the gut.
Yogurt has acidophilus to aid in digestion of the milk. All are beneficial and allowed in all seasons, if not allergic or intolerant.

What do I need to know about supplementation?
All supplements are just that—not a supplemental source of nutrition as much as supplementing the income for the alternative food and supplement industry.

You are saying that all of our nutrition should come from good quality food.
And a good quality water source to hydrate you sufficiently.

Detox Soup

I'd like to detox my body, boost my energy, and lose 2-3 pounds. How could I do it?
I am thinking of something like a diet of bone broth with celery and quinoa soup for a few days.
I just invented that idea. A thousand experts will give you a thousand different answers.
A diet of organic bone broth with lots of carrots and a little bit of Italian seasoning would detox the body, allowing all other carbohydrates and proteins to halt digestion of them, allowing a cleansing of the cells in the body.

Does this diet allow enzymes to function better to do repair work in the body?
It allows enzymes to heal in the body by not having to digest all manner of ingested materials and proteins that halt them from healing in other areas.

Add some sea salt?
A little bit, not a lot—meaning 1/2 teaspoon to 1 large pot.

For how many days, and how many meals per day should I have the carrot soup?
A daily ingestion of 1 gallon of the soup for 8 days would achieve the desired results.

How many times per year?

About every 3-4 months would be ideal, meaning in each season.

Would it be best to limit ingesting the soup to a window of 8-10 hours, say 8 AM - 6 PM?
About 15 hours of not eating is optimal in detoxification.

How about garlic or onion, or adding some kale?
A little bit of garlic is the only other ingredient allowed in the soup.

Can I drink Green Tea in the morning, and have a coffee at noon?
A cup of each is healing, so have them early in the morning, 1 hour before the detox soup.

How about wine in the evening?
A glass of healing red or white wine will allow the body an interval of halting infinite stressors, and induce better sleep.

I think I am going to like this diet. What about protein—won't I be hungry or weak?
Not as hungry or weak as most days of a normal diet.

I expect that this detox soup diet will clear my head, especially if adding a short meditation.
A meditation on having healing illumination throughout your body allows healing and detoxification an easier manifestation in the body by allowing it.

Should the carrots be shredded to be cooked or digested better?
A carrot has a life force illuminating in its original state, meaning in holding its shape.
Cut each carrot into about 4 mini carrot shapes.

Should the soup just be heated and not cooked —to not cook the life force out of the carrots?
Carrots can be cooked for 4 minutes, heating only and not boiling.

SS https://superfoodsanctuary.com › raw-carrot-salad-recipe-for-hormone-balance
Raw Carrot Salad Recipe for Hormone Balance
Just eating a single raw carrot a day is the easiest, cheapest and most natural hormone balancing remedy out there. Uncover 5 benefits of carrots for hormones and more below: 1. Estrogen Detox Effects . Dr Ray Peat, an endocrinologist found that by eating one medium-sized raw carrot every day,...

https://lifebotanica.com › what-you-should-know-detox-benefits-of-carrots-plus-recipe
Detox Benefits of Carrots | Life Botanica
In one study, carrot juice extract used for 72 hours in the treatment of leukemia stopped the progression of the disease. Another study reported that a carrot diet might help prevent prostate cancer. Adding carrots to your diet will help you achieve better health. Carrots provide many detox...

Laying on Left Side

I just heard that a wise Buddhist monk had said it is best for people to sleep on their left sides— and understand it aids lymph drainage to the left, heart pumping downhill, and spleen functioning, etc. Is that correct?

Asleep means not having awareness of how the body moves in its positioning while allowing itself an interval of sleep, so an inactive position cannot be held for very long.

A position of laying on the left side allows half of the body to be in an underlying compression force, and the other half compressing it. A compression of the left side causes all of the compressed internal organs to become alimentary canal drainage activators, meaning they are detoxifying themselves.

Amazing Benefits of Sleeping on Your Left Side | John Douillard's

2.5M views

Discover the Surprising Benefits of Sleeping on Your Left Side!

20 views

STONEHENGE

Why was Stonehenge in England built?
England had huge Giants in the era before the last era—about 800,000 years ago, until about 450,000 years ago.
They made the stone structures in 9 locations, although 8 are buried in sediment under the oceans.
All were made for holding animals in the beginning, then for housing themselves in the more inclement weather in that era.

Stonehenge

Did they live in other structures besides stone structures?
All had homes in the ground, and only 9 were above ground.

Why were the 9 built above ground?
All held their most important hunted animal, the mammoth elephant.

How big were the Giants?
About 15'-18' in height, and weighing almost 1,000 pounds.

Did they populate most of the Earth?
Almost all of Europe in that era, including areas under the Atlantic Ocean; large portions of Asia and Africa, also including submerged portions; likewise in the North and South American continents.

For how many years did the Giants populate the Earth?
About 5,000 years.

How long did a Giant typically live?
All had the potential to live about 50 years, but most lived about 40 years or less.

What else can you tell me about them?
All Giants had keen fighting abilities, and fought each other to the death—meaning they doomed themselves as a species.

Did they have low intelligence?
About as intelligent as an alligator, or a lizard.

At the peak of their population, how many were living on the Earth?
About 4 million in the largest population in that era.

It still took enormous strength to move and lift the 13' high stones at Stonehenge.
All were lifted by about 20 Giants.

I suppose that alligators could be very intelligent, and I've seen people function with

the intellectual curiosity of a lizard—but how were the Giants able to build Stonehenge with low intelligence?

Alligators catch fish in their mouths without having to move, allowing them not to exert energy.

Giants had large rocks in their location that could be handled in the construction of the corrals, meaning holding animals so they did not have to hunt for food. A Giant's brain could calculate hunting vs. corralling, and chose hunting to corral—providing food for the winter.

Corralling meant finding stones that were higher than they were wide, and hauling them to the corral area.

Were the stones all found, and not cut?

All were found within 1/4 mile of the corral.

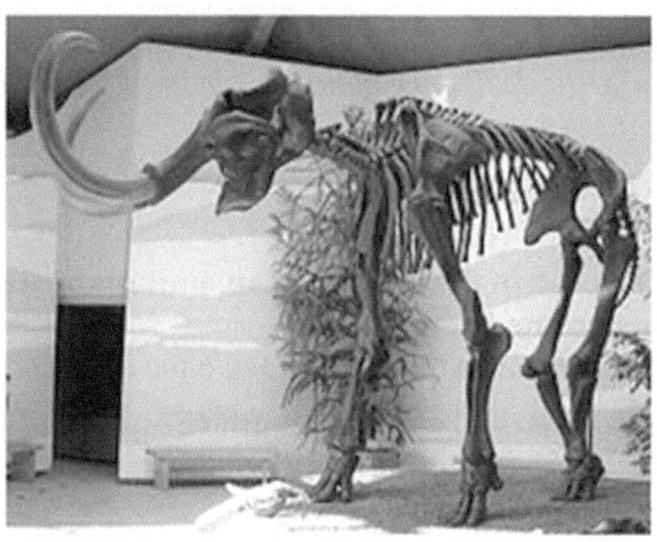

*Largest European specimen, a male Mammoth elephant.
(Public domain image)*

Museum display of Ecuadoran Giant Skeleton

Only One Variable

Are there laws of the universe?
Laws are something that can be broken; the design of the universe cannot be broken.

Are there design principles then?
A delicate design principle that has only one variable—your loving, or non-loving thoughts.

Please explain.
A healed thought is loving, and heals your universe. A non-loving thought needs to heal either in your life-mind while you are alive, or in your Light Mind when you are not physically alive.

The goal is to heal our minds while we are alive, and that is why we come here—repeatedly, correct?
Allowing all that you love is healed, and allowing all that you do not love is healing.
Allowing everything is healing in your mind, or healed in God Mind—meaning all that heals in your mind makes God Mind and your mind One.
Healed as One with God Mind allows you to manifest all you desire.

My desire right now is for God Mind to tell me something funny.
All that you allow to heal becomes a funny anecdote in my mind that had kept us apart, as you stumbled around looking for the light—and can now laugh at

yourself for being in a game of 'Pin the Tail on the Donkey'.

Okay, that was fun—I found the light with my blindfold on.
A blindfold is all the fear and guilty thoughts that halt the loving thoughts. Allow them to heal by loving them for coming to show you all that has been a joke to me, but a healing anecdote to you.

THE JOKE IS ON ME

How many times
   can one heart beat
did I say beat
   I meant to say break

and how much time
   can one heart ache
did I say ache
   I meant to say take

can it make a mistake
   and not admit defeat
why does it feel
   that it cannot be free

*It did not break
   but was only bruised
and it did not heal
   because you refused*

to see the truth
* in your reviews*
of all the times
* you did not choose*

love and peace
* and goodness would lose*
if you could see me
* you'd see I'm amused*

because when you go back
* and think about then*
do you think about you
* or think about them?*

my, oh my
* were they offended*
and couldn't take a joke
* at least not as intended*

let's send them a blessing
* when the thoughts appear*
and stop distressing
* it's not what you fear*

they forgave you
* as you forgave them*
feeling it now
* is healing it when*

the joke is on you
* because in the end*
in a cosmic sense
* I will mend*

all that was said
　and all that was done
there's no defense
　when the truth has won

so you'll have to laugh
　and I think you'll agree
if All is one
　then the joke is on me

(did I say laugh
　I should have said "gaffe"
Ha! there I go again
　gaffes from the past!)

The Most Powerful Manifesting Engine

In my last book, *The Book of Manifesting*, you said that a Merkabah is "*a flowing, healing, light-activator,*" and that it "*has healed God Mind illumination all around it and inside of it,*" and that "*a healed God Mind illumination manifests in life.*"
Should I visualize myself inside the Merkabah, and make my wish?
A light activation heals in God Mind, allowing the healed manifestation into a light hologram—or your reality.

That is totally awesome.
Awesome illuminations heal in God Mind, and flow into your reality.

Where does the Merkabah come from?
A Merkabah illuminates in the Mind of God as individuations of itself, meaning as your individuation of myself.

Is God Mind a Merkabah?
A healed illumination of itself is in a Merkabah, allowing illumination of all Merkabahs.

I can't help but think that the inside of a Merkabah is as close to God Mind as we can get.
A Merkabah is God Mind, meaning inside a Merkabah is as close to healed in life as you can get.

Isn't that the most powerful manifesting tool there is?
It allows healing in the life-mind which is the most powerful manifesting engine—healing, illuminating, and flowing God Mind inside and around it.
Activate it by holding it illuminating in your mind, making an illumination of 405 nm[2] all inside and around it.
Imagine God Mind illuminating inside and all around it, illuminating healing in the Merkabah.

So, just light it up in my mind before using it?
Activating God Mind illumination inside of it, yes. All heals in the illumination inside of it.

Should we place a light source inside of it in the center, or one in each 60-degree angle point?
A light in the center illuminates in all directions.

My friend, Jim, is building a life-size Merkabah using 6' long copper tubes. If he stands inside of it, where would the light source be?
All inside and around it, meaning wherever it can be placed.

Merkabah mysticism

Merkabah or Merkavah mysticism is a school of early Jewish mysticism, c. 100 BCE – 1000 CE, centered on visions such as those found in Ezekiel 1 or in the hekhalot literature, concerning stories of ascents to the heavenly palaces and the Throne of God. **Wikipedia**

---

[2] 405 nm light frequency, blue-magenta (see photo on back cover).

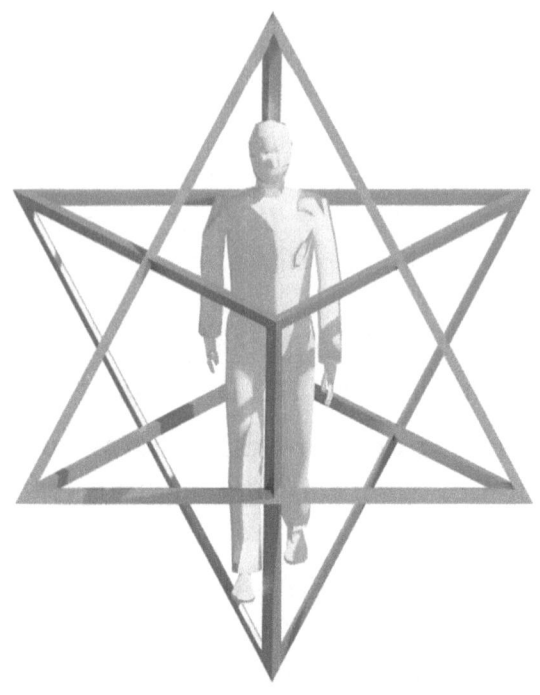

A Merkabah, artwork by Ryan Classen.

You said to make "*an illumination of 405 nm all around it.*" What is special about that light frequency?
It is the Frequency of God Mind, having God Mind illumination as its only property.

What does it do in our world of light and dark?
It allows all healing in its illumination to open in God Mind healed.

It is in the blue-magenta ultraviolet range, and appears as the beautiful blue color of the Earth and stars.
405 nm light is at the center of your Earth hologram.

Programming of a Loving Intention

I understand that our individual Merkabahs can be programmed.
All Merkabahs allow illuminating, activating, and programming of a loving intention.

Do I just illuminate it in my mind with 405 nm light, and then program it with my intention?
Yes, healing the illuminated intention.

Can you suggest some Merkabah programs that would be good for me?
A healing intention for loving your life, illuminating in your life-mind, allows healed manifestations into reality.

I read that it cannot be done for another person, only for yourself.
All heals in your mind only, so yes.

Does a Merkabah put us in another dimension?
A higher dimension, meaning illumination in Dimensions 4, 5, and 6.

How would we go from Dimension 4 to 6?
A dimension illuminates in the life-mind, healing higher in dimension as the life-mind heals—meaning illuminating higher in the dimensions of illuminated beings.

Is the Merkabah a vehicle that takes a person to higher dimensions?
All Merkabahs allow life-minds to heal, illuminating itself in higher dimensions—so healing is the illuminating energy that moves the Merkabah higher.

I guess I could program my Merkabah to heal my mind—and to only allow peace, love, health, abundance, and God Mind goodness into my life.
All heal, flowing and manifesting in your life— meaning all illuminate in God Mind, allowed into your mind, opening in reality.

So be it.
A flowing, healing, illumination of it.

Can you please tell me the significance of the Merkabah shape?
God Mind heals in the angles illuminating. All of the Merkabah angles correspond to the life-mind's chakras in and around the body.

How many chakras do we have?
Eight, meaning illuminating in the Number of love.[3]

For Jim, who is building a large Merkabah to get into, what is the optimal length for each tetrahedron edge, not counting the connectors?
All of the edges illuminate highest in the length of 5'-8".

---

[3] Discussed on page 109 of *The Book of Manifesting*.

Illumination of Your Desires

Can a large Merkabah be enhanced with a crystal grid, or a piece of quartz in each of the 8 points?
A Merkabah illuminates God Mind, not enhanceable.

I read in 2 more books that the Merkabah tetrahedrons spin in opposite directions. Is that incorrect?
Not incorrect, infinitely impossible.

What do you mean?
The Merkabah has 2 tetrahedrons that illuminate from an immovable source, meaning God Mind which is not moving. Motion is illusory, allowing healing in motioning toward Oneness.

What else can you tell me about the Merkabah?
All Merkabahs have a large 55' radius field of energy that holds each person's hologram in its matrix.
Life illuminates in each Merkabah that is in contact with the energy torus.[4]

Can a person bilocate by moving or illuminating their Merkabah somewhere else?
Yes, illumination can be held open in 2 or more locations. God Mind illuminates in all locations, meaning allowing more locations to open will illuminate in the illusion.

---

[4] Explained in the next chapter.

I am going to surprise the inner-earth beings by appearing there.
Illuminating in the inner-earth will not work because of the inverted physics there.[5]

Do animals have Merkabahs?
Animals, plants, and all living things illuminate in a Merkabah.

I programmed my Merkabah with affirmations such as being in the right place at the right time, allowing only peace, love, abundance, health, and God Mind goodness into it, etc.
Illumination of your desires is the Merkabah's function.

How would you define its function?
A light-activated God Mind illumination in the hologram of life, allowing itself a time and place illusion to heal in.

It is light-activated by me, correct?
Activated by you, illuminated by God Mind.

What happens to a person's Merkabah if they have non-loving thoughts about anything?
Their Merkabah illumination dims. Allowing non-love always dims a Merkabah, meaning it halts the manifesting of their desires.

---

[5] Discussed in *Mysteries, Prophecies, and the Hollow Earth.*

Wow—I mean, Ow.
All healing illuminates, or it is not healing—meaning illumination dims, and dimming is not illuminating your desires.

Excerpts from 'A Merkabah'
The Book of Manifesting

A Merkabah is a flowing, healing, light-activator.

A Merkabah has healed God Mind illumination all around it and inside of it.

A healed God Mind illumination manifests in life.

All Merkabah energy has life-mind knowledge illuminating healed all around it and inside of it—healed in God Mind.

Imagine being healed, illuminating inside of one.

God Mind healing halts non-love, activating life-mind healing... healing the mind in about a minute.

A Merkabah illuminates God Mind in your mind, allowing healing illumination.

All illuminating in the Frequency of God Mind (405 nm light) and in a Merkabah, circle in a feedback loop into God Mind healed, and into the Light Mind healed.

Healed in God Mind Instantly

Please correct or add to my instructions for someone to use the Merkabah.

1. Picture yourself inside of the Merkabah looking out.
Acclimating higher or lower to fit inside of it.

2. Activate it by visualizing the God Mind frequency of 405 nm blue light all around and inside of it.
Activate it by illuminating it, making the illumination increase in intensity to God Mind infinite lightness.

3. Program the Merkabah with your wishes for things that are good.
And hold the almost healed desires in the Merkabah's center, near the heart.
Love the desire healing in God Mind.

4. Notice the healed desires effortlessly manifesting in reality.
Allow healed desires illumination in the hologram of life.

Is that everything?
All healed in God Mind is everything, so yes.

What about the breath?
Allow breaths to inhale on your wish, and exhale on it healing.

Do the wishes heal instantly?
All heal in God Mind instantly, meaning in a God Mind moment of loving its creation.

You said that "*Life illuminates in each Merkabah that is in contact with the energy torus.*" What is the energy torus?
An energy center has an energy field acclimating itself to other energy fields, allowing all energy fields to cooperate. Energy fields have an apple-shaped torus all around them that flows back into itself.

An energy torus has only one property, and that is what you give to it.

Like what?
A loving property heals with the energy torus, and non-love has no healing affect—but on the contrary, non-love prevents the torus from healing all other energy fields in the hologram.

That's the opposite of what we want, since we are here to heal, and need to heal to manifest, etc.
All energy fields allow you to heal with their assistance.

The Earth Merkabah

Most people don't want hateful violence. How could we eliminate it on a global scale?
Imagine halting non-love in an Earth Merkabah, making it illuminate in healing and love.

Does the Earth have a Merkabah?
All life has a Merkabah, making the Earth's Merkabah the largest in the Earth hologram.

If I activate, illuminate, and program the Earth's Merkabah, will it make a significant difference?
A difference illuminates in the life-minds on Earth, meaning loving themselves more.
Loving themselves more makes the Merkabahs of each individual illuminate more.
Illumination of each individual's Merkabah halts non-love, allowing loving thoughts and actions.

Will most of the people on Earth allow it in their minds?
All will illuminate in their Merkabahs; healing illumination enters their minds, and a lightness will envelope humanity.

I know this is just my dream of love and light, so let's lighten it up.
A dream of healing means illumination works for all.

Healing my mind raises mass consciousness, but would a top down approach be more powerful—to illuminate the Earth's Merkabah, and illuminate everyone in it that way?
All who illuminate in the Earth's hologram illuminate their Merkabahs from the Earth's Merkabah illumination.

Is the Earth Merkabah the Master Merkabah?
Illuminating the Earth hologram, yes.

At the very center of the Earth hologram is 405 nm frequency light, correct?
Illuminating the hologram and all Merkabahs in it as the Frequency[6] of God Mind, yes.

The Earth Merkabah, artwork by Ryan Classen.

---

[6] Discussed on page 78 of *The Book of Manifesting*.

Can one person illuminate the Earth's Merkabah and halt non-love?
All who allow illumination in their minds will heal in the illumination of the Earth's Merkabah.

By what percentage will non-love be reduced on the planet?
About 25 or 26 percent.

What if several people do it, and keep doing it?
All non-love heals in the illumination of the Earth's Merkabah, so eventually illumination halts all non-love.

Coinciding with the coming New Age or the next era?[7]
Yes.

---

[7] Discussed in later chapters.

God Mind Recognition of Itself

Are there energy centers on the Earth that correspond to the points of the Earth's Merkabah?
Yes, 8 points of energy highly illuminating, meaning healing energy vortices on the Earth's grid of ley lines. Healing illuminates in the highly energized vortices as God Mind illuminating life-minds.

Does the Earth rotate inside of a stationary Merkabah, or do they both move together?
All Merkabahs move in unison with their host life forms.

Where are the healing energy vortices on the Earth?
At the North and South Poles are 2 of them, 4 are in the oceans, 1 is in Russian territory, and 1 is in the jungles of Brazil.

What would it do to a person the be at one of the vortices?
It heals them in an instant of God Mind recognition of itself in everything.

What about being on one of the ley lines connecting them?
It would be similar, but not as illuminating.

How wide is a ley line?
Lines only have one dimension in their length.

Is there a ley line near here?
About 550 miles away is the nearest line from you.

Is there a great retirement location that happens to be on a ley line?
Ajijic, Mexico is on a ley line.

I understand that it is a beautiful, magical town.
Ajijic has healing properties in its vortex, magically illuminating its residents.

It has a vortex also?
A vortex illuminates in each person's Merkabah that is at the intersection of the Earth, sky, and a ley line on the Earth.

What does that do?
A vortex halts all non-love, meaning it illuminates God Mind.

That explains the magical illumination and healing.
All healing illumination in God Mind is magical.

It would also allow a person to magically manifest their desires.
All that are healed in God Mind, and allowed by the life-mind, yes.

Ajijic, Mexico

As Healed as a Person Can Get

In *The Book of Manifesting*, there is a chapter on structuring water that starts on p. 251.
We had discussed illuminating God Mind in water by running it through a 14" long piece of 2" diameter bamboo, filled with river stones. You said it is *"a healing filter from nature"*, and it *"eliminates the 5 main energies adversely affecting humanity—#1 Avarice, #2 Greed, #3 Hatred, #4 Envy, #5 Decadence."*

Can the 14" bamboo tube be enhanced by carving the number 8 on it, or other geometric symbols?
All will hold open in illumination of its attributes.

What would be the best symbol for structuring water?
Any attribute that you engrave will illuminate into the bamboo flowform and in the water.

Which symbols do you suggest?
Love in the number 8 is one, and healing illuminates in the hexagonal shape.

What can you tell me about water that is structured, and then enhanced with the number 8 and a hexagonal shape?

Alternating between God Mind and the life-mind halting non-love—it illuminates in both of them, meaning it heals the life-mind instantly.

That would then heal the body, correct?
A healed mind allows the illumination of its body, so yes.

What if I drink the healed water and stand inside of a life-size Merkabah illuminated with 405 nm light, the Frequency of God Mind?
Inside a Merkabah is as healed in the life-mind as a person can get, so illuminating and adding healed water illuminates the illumination—meaning it illuminates in God Mind instantly and infinitely, or never ending.

Would that heal my other lifetimes—or what I would call past lives and future lives?
All in one instant, opening them in God Mind, yes.

How would all of the lifetimes change?
All heal in God Mind, meaning they illuminate in love; healing manifestations in them to open in reality.

It sounds like all of my past and future lives will benefit significantly. How will my life change now?
All lifetimes illuminate in God Mind now, so healing all of them illuminates in your mind now—healed in God Mind eternally.

What does that mean? Are my lifetimes complete?

Not complete until your agreements are fulfilled—meaning completing book writing for humans to heal in reading them, yes.

This information will put me on the fast track to heal this illusion.

A dream of healing, illuminating in your mind—now not dreaming, awakened in God Mind healed, yes.

Am I "*awakened in God Mind healed*"?

All are awake when asleep, and are dreaming when they are not sleeping. Being healed in God Mind means awakening in the dream of life, and allowing it to heal by your allowing it to heal in your acceptance and love of all life. Allow and accept life by loving all of it.

An Alkaline Body

Is there something that would heal a body of cancer?
All cancers have one common denominator—an acidic body.
All cancers healing have one thing in common—an alkaline body.

The remedy wouldn't really cost much, and could even save money to eliminate toxic media, sugar, artificial sweeteners and soda, food preservatives and GMO's, fluoride, chemicals, and EMF's...
Adding a little bit of lemon to drinking water is alkalizing also.

Could someone with an advanced or aggressive cancer heal it by alkalizing their body with green juicing, detoxifying as we had previously discussed, plus standing on the Earth in bare feet, etc.?
And eliminating all mRNA effects by taking Ivermectin in mineral water also.[8]

Do particular foods have an anti-cancer effect?
Apricot seeds, almonds, and blueberries decimate cancer cells with active ingredients they contain.

Blueberries are especially good for alkalizing also.

---

[8] Discussed on page 66.

Blueberries are considered a superfood and have shown potential cancer-fighting properties. They contain many antioxidants and other cancer-fighting compounds, including anthocyanosides, resveratrol, flavonoids, and proanthocyanidins:

- Anthocyanosides: One of the most potent antioxidants, anthocyanosides may reduce cell proliferation and inflammation, and stimulate detoxifying enzymes
- Resveratrol: Also found in red grape skin, resveratrol has many health benefits
- Flavonoids and proanthocyanidins: These brightly colored compounds may affect cell growth and death, and fight free radicals

Some studies have shown that blueberries may help prevent cell damage linked to cancer, and may have other effects, such as:

- Controlling tumor growth
- Decreasing metastasis
- Inducing cell death in triple-negative breast cancer cells
- Inhibiting cancer cell survival and growth
- Decreasing inflammatory cytokines
- Decreasing estrogen-induced mammary cancer
- Decreasing DNA damage

Some studies have found that eating almonds and other tree nuts may help reduce the risk of certain cancers, including:

Colorectal cancer

A Yale Cancer Center study found that colon cancer survivors who ate two or more servings of tree nuts per week were 46% less likely to have the cancer return. Preclinical studies also suggest that mixed nuts, including almonds, may inhibit DNA damage and tumor growth.

Breast cancer

One study found that high consumption of almonds may reduce the risk of breast cancer by 2-3 times.

"As to the diet, to keep the body-building forces ... in the afternoon [middle of the afternoon] eat half an ounce of almonds; just almonds..."

—Edgar Cayce Reading 954-2

A client, Kim asked me about her recurring cancer.
All becomes healing in her mind as she accepts her cancer diagnosis, and then heals it.

What is causing it?
A cancer has a heart and mind of its own, meaning it cannot be healed if it is hated—only if it is accepted, and it is healed with love in time.

Affirm this: "Cancer heal in all that I love—my body, my heart, and my mind. I love them and heal them all—instantly in my mind, infinitely in my heart, and timely in my body. Heal all cancer that I do not desire, and I do not have a need for in my love of life, God, and myself."

Activation of a Mental Pain

Cancer is an epidemic, and I have had melanoma several times. Even if there is an environmental cause, isn't it manifested from a mental source?
All cancers are caused by a mental activation of a mental pain that becomes a physical ailment.

Can they all be healed mentally?
Affirm, "All that I am activating in my body that is cancerous is allowed to heal, and all of my mental pains heal in my allowing them, and forgiving them."

"I ask angels to take all of my mental pains to God Mind where they immediately heal into light."
Affirming it will allow angels to connect to God Mind.

Another poem comes to mind, "Now They Are Light."
Allow the poem to heal all non-loving memories of guilt or shame.

Now They Are Light

I confess
  I was not at my best
the dozens of times
  when I failed the test

and went out of my lane
   out of my league
no one to blame
   only me

maybe the poem
   should end right here
along with the shame
   the same every year

What you can do
   to be truly healed
is to take your regrets
   how you truly feel

roll them up tight
   shrink-wrapped and sealed
hold them in the light
   no need to kneel

You can have them
   just let me know
I've added a label
   they are ready to go

I will recycle
   transmute and shift
repurpose and repackage
   what you have shipped

they were kind of heavy
   but that's alright
I have healed them with love
   now they are light

My understanding is that guilt and shame are the two most destructive feelings—enough to make a person sick.
Affirm, "All the guilt and all of the shame are all with God and heal all my pain."

You're a poet too!
Actually, I am the co-author of your poetry, so yes. All heal in their minds when reading it.

So, to heal cancer, I would personally detox with bone broth, alkalize the body, ask angels to connect my mental pains to God Mind where they cannot exist in the light, then I would say the affirmations, and ask angels to change the frequency of my body to its ideal.
All will activate healing in the body, and not allow cancer a home there.

Easy, right?
All healing is easy, you only have to allow it.

What else should I include to share with readers?
Acclimate all of your thoughts to God Mind by affirming, "God Mind is all that I am."

God Mind is all that I am. That changes everything.
All that I am doesn't change. Allow yourself to be God Mind not changing.

"I am God Mind. Everything that changes is healing, and I allow it to heal."
Affirm it, live it, and love it.

An Energetic Adjustment

I learned about frequencies when studying dowsing, which is technically known as 'radiesthesia' for receiving information, and 'radionics' for sending information, or distance healing. Adjusting a person's frequency to its ideal frequency has resulted in their spontaneous remission from cancer. I did it dozens of times—silently asking for permission, then not mentioning it. The story below is a good example.

In October 2005, my father said his cousin Marie in Ireland was diagnosed with breast cancer. With the pendulum and a numerical chart, I checked her frequency and asked if she had cancer, then confirmed, "Yes, she has cancer. I will show you how to clear it—it's easy."

I silently asked if it was okay to do healing for Marie, and then adjusted her frequency to its ideal. My dowsing showed that she was cancer-free.

A spirit message I received at the time said, "Yes, she is cancer free. She feels like she is not alone in this anymore."

Two months later in December 2005, my father received a Christmas card from Marie with a note. "I am cancer free. I feel like I am not alone in this anymore."

Ten years later, in 2015, Marie's daughter came to Virginia and said that the doctors were very surprised that Marie has lived more than 5 years because her 2005 diagnosis was Stage 4 and the cancer had spread to her lymph glands at that time—of which I was unaware. Then in 2017, 12 years after the diagnosis and my energy healing, I met Marie in Virginia when she came to visit. I still did not think it was necessary to mention the energy healing I had done in 2005. She passed away in 2018.

Can adjusting a person's frequency energetically heal them?
An energetic adjustment can heal a person instantly in their mind, and in a nano-second or more in their body.

How does an energetic adjustment help them?
Adjusting a person's frequency can open DNA portals, allowing access to God Mind energy, healing them.

Simple enough. Can't every person easily do it for themselves?
Yes, asking for their frequency to be adjusted to their ideal is accomplished by asking angels to heal their frequency by adjusting it in their DNA portals.

I understand that our DNA portals open, or close, to Oneness or God Mind on the other side.
Opening and closing the portals depends on our loving or non-loving thoughts, respectively.

All of life has DNA, and DNA portals to God Mind wisdom, allowing all life to hear God Mind in their stillness.

Is there an affirmation a person could use to adjust the frequency of their DNA portals to heal themselves?
Affirm this, "Angels, adjust my frequency to heal all of my DNA, allowing God Mind to heal in my mind, allowing my body to heal."

That will do it.
Allowing it will do it.

What would prevent a person from allowing it?
Accepting that loving themselves allows it—is what will do it.

An Investment Has 8 Characteristics

Is Bitcoin a good investment?
An investment has 8 characteristics:

- *it has enduring dealing interest*
- *it advances its holder's gaining wealth*
- *it advances in investment value at no additional expense*
- *it advances in holding onto its value in all market conditions*
- *it has alternate uses other than for trading*
- *it cannot be degraded over time by the elements*
- *it has immediate international recognition*
- *alternate or increasing amounts cannot be introduced*

Bitcoin can meet many, but not all of these characteristics. Holding it is invisible. A Bitcoin is held in an account in an infrastructure that needs a computer and electricity.

A better, indestructible investment is Gold—although Gold has a limited number of markets it can be traded in.

Gold holds its investment value in any market condition, does not corrode, and can be held in your hand.

I don't own any Gold, just some Silver—and some freeze-dried food for survival if I ever need it.

All can be exchanged for what you will anticipate having a need for in the future.

What will I need in the future?

A distiller of water that is solar powered.

Why will I need that?

All power systems will not be operational in the decades that follow the poles' shifting. Fresh water will be the most desired commodity.

When will that be?

Water will be the most desired commodity in 12 more years.

Because of the "*poles' shifting*"?

Because of their initial geomagnetic repositioning, yes.

An Alien Entity

Am I delusional, or is the government trying to kill or impoverish everyone?
An alien entity that controls the government leaders accesses their hatefulness, and directs their thoughts to enact hateful and destructive legislation for most people.

The devil entities are energized by hateful violence.

Okay, good. I didn't think I was delusional.
A-D-D maybe, but allowed to be deficit in attention to the life-mind.

A Conundrum of Love and Non-love

I find myself—or I placed myself—in a collapsing empire, where many people expect for it to end very badly, in bankruptcy and death, and it seems that the government is actively and intentionally accelerating it.
Can I change that dream, or only my personal outcome in the dream?
An interactive dream has an infinite number of outcomes, all healing in their ending the illusion of dreaming.
A healed illusion has only one outcome, meaning healing in God Mind as the awakened dreamer.
'Awakened' doesn't allow a lack of healing, or a lack of perfection in its eternal God Mind.
Do not allow healing an instance of relapsing into fearfulness, or hatefulness in others to bring you back into the dream.

Thank you, because I was thinking that even if I had a healed mind, I could get swept up in social chaos and upheaval.
All healed in God Mind cannot be chaotic or in an upheaval, meaning all that you can experience is blissfulness and contentment—although others may not have the same experience.

So, the whole dream will not change except for my experience in it?

The actualizations in the dream will change, actualizing a harmonious outcome for you.

Whoa—that's really cool—so there is nothing to be afraid of.
Actualizing fears, halting love, allows the dream to become a nightmare or hellscape. Fear actualizes things to fear.
Non-love is fearing love, actualizing more non-love in your life.

Please tell me about the actualization process.
A dream has an actualization component, meaning a fear or love mechanism activated by your healed or unhealed thoughts about life and others in it. A loving thought activates healing in your mind, meaning a loving thought heals, allowing healed God Mind manifestations in the dreamscape. Fear halts loving thoughts—not healing them in God Mind, and not allowing manifestations healed in God Mind. Not healing fears actualizes a hellscape or a nightmare in allowing them to manifest what you are fearing.

I guess that sums it up—I'll get what I love, and also what I fear?
A conundrum of love and non-love in the same mind—meaning you can't have both to heal the mind.

Non-love has to go.
Non-love has to heal.

And I will actualize a beautiful dream of a life.
A beautiful dream actualizing God Mind in a life.

conundrum /kə-nŭn'drəm/

noun

A paradoxical, insoluble, or difficult problem; a dilemma

Only One Antidote

April 2024–How many people worldwide died as a direct result of the Covid shots in the last 4 years?
Almost 61 million.

How many people were partially or fully disabled from it?
About 500 million willingly allowing an injection altered to maim or kill, maiming more in the next 2 years than in the last 4 years—meaning increasing fatalities also.

Was the injection intended to have a delayed effect?
An immediate effect with delayed debilitation.

How long after the shot, or when will the death rate peak?
Allowing for different injection dates, death finds all within 10 years of injection—unless injected more than once, and death comes within 5 years.

Was the shot perfected before they deployed it?
Not perfected, but diabolically infected.

What was it designed to do?
Alter the mind of the injected to not love itself, giving it instructions to power down different organs.

Is the injected substance given instructions and activated from an external source?
All of the instructions illuminate in the screens of cell phones, allowing the light to instill the programs in peoples' eyes who look at them.

Are signals sent randomly, or are certain people or phone numbers targeted?
Both, meaning instilling the programs can target millions of people in thousands of ways to have nothing noticeable in their environments changed.

What if someone is older and doesn't have a cell phone, is the Covid injection still harmful, or is it inactivated?
A Covid injection has light-limiting properties in it, meaning it can allow non-light into the organs which cause them to become cancerous.

What can a person do to counteract the mRNA effect, or to disable the shot?
The mRNA injection has only one antidote—mineral water that has Ivermectin in it. A dosage of 18 mg (1-1/2 tablets) every day for 2 weeks will alter the mRNA injection, disabling its light-limiting properties. All heal in time, allowing their organs to make new cells that are not instilled with mRNA.

One common denominator among myself and friends who could see the obvious vax scam is that we don't watch TV. Were people affected mostly by fear from listening to 'news', or from a subliminal messaging component on TV?

All network television programming has a low frequency messaging component that effectively hijacks a person's imagination.
Imagination forms thoughts from perceptions.

Is it brainwashing?
A brainwashing can only enter the brain if allowed to enter.

Can TV brainwashing be undone?
All brainwashing can be halted in an instant by eliminating illegitimate stimulation of the left-brain hemisphere of the brain.
Eliminating illegitimate stimulation includes instilling natural and loving stimulations.

It was pretty obvious that nothing about the Covid vaccine scam was right. At the time I said, "The whole thing stinks."
- approved on a Friday and 100 million doses ready on Monday?... They must have worked on it all weekend.
- Congress and Post Office workers exempt?...if it was so great, shouldn't they be first?
- millions of immigrants exempt?
- shots were approved for experimental use. Doesn't the Nuremburg Code forbid medical experimentation on people?
- doctors who spoke out faced losing their medical licenses.
- medical journals published lies and fabricated articles.

- truth-tellers were harshly censored, and deplatformed.
- Ivermectin was ridiculed as "horse paste". Why was it awarded a Nobel Prize for treatment of infectious diseases?
- the definition of 'vaccine' was downgraded from "provides immunity" to "offers protection." Vitamin C, D, and zinc do that.
- "Trust the science." I do trust the science which says the shots are neither safe, nor effective—on the contrary.
- initial company vaccine trials were disastrous. Why does the FDA not want their data released for 75 years?
- the risk of dying from Covid was wildly exaggerated. Why were hospitals paid to label deaths from other causes as Covid deaths?
- vaccines and masks were mandated. What is a mandate? Did we vote it into law?

w https://en.wikipedia.org › wiki › COVID-19_vaccination_mandates_in_the_United_States
COVID-19 vaccination mandates in the United States - Wikipedia
Federal mandates. In September 2021, Biden announced the Biden administration COVID-19 action plan, a six-point plan of new measures to help control the pandemic, which included new executive orders and regulatory actions to effectively mandate vaccination for COVID-19 among a large swath o...

Why were billions of people around the world pressured, coerced, or frightened into taking the shots?
Altering the DNA of people gives controlling parties the highest amount of half control, and half murder ability in their manipulations.

Is their goal to decrease the world population?
In a steady rate of decline, yes.

By how much and how soon?
A 50 percent reduction in 10 years is the first goal, and 80 percent in 20 years is the second goal.

Do they think they are saving the planet by eliminating most of the people?
All halt loving thoughts for others because they are infected with an entity from the far end of the galaxy.

What we would call the devil.
An alien entity that defiles human minds, not permitting light to enter. All heal in life or in losing their life, meaning in death.

What percentage of humans have their minds controlled by this entity?
Almost 18 percent, including most leaders of large governments.

The Devil Entity

Please tell me about the devil entity from the far end of the Milky Way Galaxy.
A devil enters into life-minds that invite it in, defiling their life-minds—meaning it eliminates light in their minds to almost non-existent in many instances.

Is it invited into the minds of political figures who participate in Satanic rituals such as at Bohemian Grove?
Allowing it in halts love in their minds, so illumination no longer functions—leaving them pure evil in their entity controlled minds.

It seems to have spread throughout our culture.
It defiles human minds, entering in their halting love for one another—making them think they are more powerful than others, including God Mind.

Bohemian Grove
Private men's club in California
bohemianclub.com/home/bohemian-grove

Bohemian Grove is a restricted 2,700-acre campground in Monte Rio, California. Founded in 1878, it belongs to a private gentlemen's club known as the Bohemian Club. In mid-July each year, Bohemian Grove hosts a more than two-week encampment of some of the most prominent men in the world. Wikipedia

Can the devil entity enter peoples' minds inadvertently, or does it need to be invited to enter?

Allowing it is inviting it, so any joy from violence in peoples' minds invites it.

Movies, TV entertainment, and video games are saturated with violence—as well as TV news; mainly a reflection of the government's dishonest and malicious actions and aggression—not occasionally, but all the time as a matter of policy.

All dishonesty and actions of hateful violence alter the life-mind's illumination to be lowered, darkening it to the point of not having loving thoughts.

Has it reached a tipping point in our society where it seems that hate and dishonesty are what is driving it?

Allowing it allows more of it. Illegal and illegitimate governments hate not only their own people, but all people including themselves.

This devil entity—what would it look like if I could see it?

A half humanoid and half monster creature with long horns, halting light in its presence.

I'm sure Hollywood has depicted it accurately in their presentations, having direct inspiration from it.

A large, hateful, monster creature halting loving thoughts is in the minds of most leaders of countries, large organizations, and large corporations that influence the media.

It seems that a devil-controlled mind is a prerequisite for a 'leadership' role here.
Illegitimate leadership halting love is only a prerequisite for losing God Mind connection, meaning losing all goodness in your lifetime.

Can this devil entity be eliminated from our planet with light, or angels, etc.?
Yes, illuminating each life-mind in loving itself will eliminate it.
Life-minds eliminating non-love will allow illumination that it despises.

It's not very likely to happen then.
After all people die, it no longer has life-minds to defile on the Earth.

When would that be?
Illumination of the planet hologram ceases in about 28 more years in a geomagnetic reversal.

And the game is over.
Allowing the Earth to heal itself in a period of purification, and start a new era.

Where did humanity go wrong?
In allowing hateful information and images in the media, pornography closing peoples' hearts, and hating life in the most illogical way—meaning hating one's self, and blaming God who is one's self.

Could a mass exorcism remove the devil entity from the planet?
Not remove it, but heal it in illumination, yes.

How many people would it take to accomplish this?
Not more than 3,000 people would be needed to illuminate the entity into the light—meaning into a healed state of loving itself.

Hating it probably makes it stronger in its darkness, and illuminating it would eliminate its darkness.
Hating anything makes one's self darker, so yes.

Let's say 3,000 people focused on illuminating it. What would happen?
It would heal into lightness, allowing life-minds to illuminate in lightness also.

The Earth hologram will illuminate brighter, so maybe it won't weaken and flip the poles?
Illogically, it will intensify the hologram and hasten the pole reversal because the entity is the inverse of lightness—meaning light needs non-light to exist.

You are right—when the illusion of duality ends, there is only Oneness.
Making illusions disappear is the goal.

A Non-love Repellant

**My friend, Jim, was dismayed by your last response—that the light in our planet hologram needs non-light to exist.
My reply to him was "...choose another planet next time, but then again, where's the challenge?"**
A light/non-light planetary hologram allowing love/non-love is the only hologram that can heal itself in its illumination, or love.

Please explain.
A light hologram illuminates in all directions. Non-light, or non-love is not illuminating—only allowed to exist as an illusion of non-light, or its shadow. All shadows disappear in lightness, or love.

Shadows are non-light, coldness is non-heat, non-love is an absence of love, which does not exist in God Mind.
All heal in heating or illuminating, meaning in loving that is allowed by the life-mind.

What is our challenge?
A challenge is allowing them, and illuminating them.

Was this devil entity invited in because it is needed for light to exist?
A devil entity halting love has been invited into each mind that it inhabits, making itself an illogical home in an Earth hologram of light and love.

Is the devil entity uncomfortable being in life-minds on the Earth?
Not uncomfortable, feeling unwelcome in the illumination of the Earth and all of nature.

Are plants and animals void of non-love?
All of nature loves life, meaning loves itself—meaning it does not allow non-love in its Light Mind.

Does the devil entity have a name?
'Lucifer' is the name given by life-minds.

Is Lucifer connected with all non-loving thoughts and actions?
All hateful and illegitimate violence.

Besides love and lightness, is there something that repels Lucifer, or at least shields us from 'hateful violence'?
All Geranium flowers have a non-love repellent in their fragrance.

Maybe that's why they were traditionally planted in window boxes.
And along front entrance walks, yes.

Please Allow Me to Introduce Myself

You mentioned the entity we call 'Lucifer'. Does Lucifer have a message to share with the humans of Earth?

"Please allow me to introduce myself. I am Lucifer, a non-light being from the far end of the Milky Way Galaxy.

All light is anathema to me. A half humanoid, and half monster in appearance—I am allowed, and even invited into the minds of people on Earth, halting love in their thoughts.

All non-love is my energy source, allowing me to live until humanity dies off. I know I am contributing to my own loss of life also. More devils have incarnated on the Earth now than ever before, meaning the darkness halting loving thoughts is greater than ever. All devils halt loving thoughts in mostly powerful people in the media or in politics, allowing them to harm millions of people without caring."

I understand that you feel unwelcome on Earth, where all of nature loves life and loves itself—only humans can hate life and themselves.

"All humans halt loving thoughts in different ways. Most are harmless indiscretions on their part.

All halt loving and accepting themselves, almost always in moments of insecurity."

All allowing and inviting Lucifer into their minds allow evil into their lives, meaning they block light from entering it.

A person blocking light in his or her life has lost it. Losing light in life means losing life's purpose of moving toward Oneness.

Is this message being related to me from God Mind/ Oneness?

A lot of it is, and part is from Lucifer.

I trust that is okay for me if I am acting as a scribe.

Lucifer's scribe—making others think of a possession—is not harmful to you.

I work on increasing my light, so it may be harmful to Lucifer.

A light Lucifer can shield from.

Lucifer said that "more devils have incarnated on Earth now." Are they incarnated as people?

All inhabit human bodies and hate humanity—and life in a half-light body.

How many devils are there on Earth now?

541.

Do they all have powerful roles?

All have large corporation and government leadership roles.

Why are there so many now?

All hate humanity and halt love in their minds, so incarnating now in the End Times is entertaining.

Would they be willing to leave the planet? Laws of the Universe may prohibit interference with our destiny.

Humanity has chosen its destiny; devils are joining in their hatred and self-destruction.

When did humanity choose hateful self-destruction?

Early in the last century with creating the Federal Reserve system.

Let me guess—the Fed is a parasite that produces nothing and robs everyone's wealth and productivity, keeping them dependent and as debt slaves, and enables the government to fund continuous illegal wars that have killed millions... while squandering the nation's wealth as foolishly as possible—funding illegal bioweapons, vaccine scams, its own border invasion, censorship of the truth, aerial spraying, fabricated terror, propaganda, election interference... that's just against its own citizens, not to mention the nefarious activities, assassinations, climate engineering, and wars all over the world.

An enslavement system that will destroy the economy, and halt productivity in the destruction of the currency.

And I always thought the Fed was run by a baboon typing zeros on a laptop.

A baboon has more sense than to destroy life's advantages it has acquired.

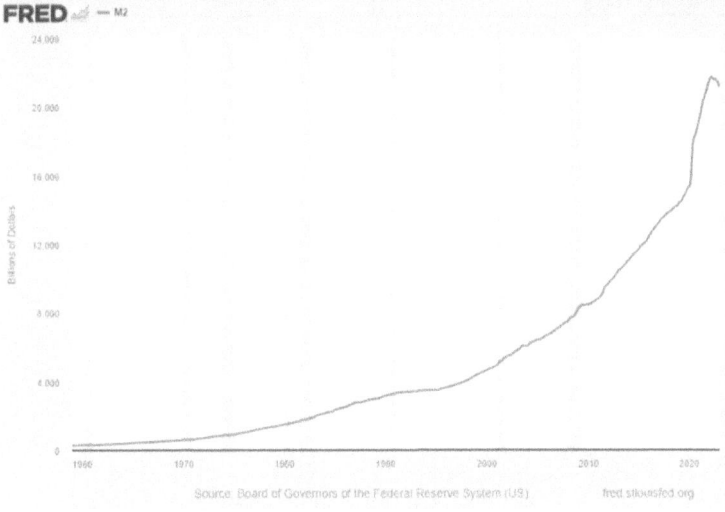

M2 Money Supply (1960-2020)

The Titanic

Did the Titanic ship sink because it hit an iceberg?
No, explosions in the engine room where a bomb had been placed prior to the voyage caused the hull to rupture and break apart.

Who wanted it to sink?
Allowing the Titanic to sink meant the bankers in New York would not lose their grip on government.

> So if why would the titanic be blown up? Well it turns out the industrialists opposed to the creation of the federal reserve were on that ship:
>
> 1. John Jacob Astor IV
> 2. Benjamin Guggenhei
> 3. Isidor Straus
> 4. George Dunton Widene
>
> This is even mentioned in the movie Titanic, in one scene, were there are a group of people arguing against the creation of the federal reserve. It's extremely short, a few seconds, but it's there.

> J.P. Morgan owned the Titanic through his trust. He was also scheduled to be a passenger for the disastrous maiden voyage but canceled at the last minute, supposedly because he was having trouble getting artwork shipped with him. This excuse seems feeble considering how much art was already on the ship, but we may never know the truth there.

🔗 https://www.npr.org › 2017 › 01 › 04 › 508242179 › titanic-documentary-suggests-engine-room-fi

Titanic Documentary Suggests Engine Room Fire Led To Sinking

Jan 4, 2017   NPR's Audie Cornish speaks with Senan Molony about his documentary, which presents evidence that a fire in the engine room could have also led to the sinking of the ship and the loss of 1,500 lives.

RMS Titanic

On the Agenda

People are wondering why their electricity bills have tripled lately. The cost of homes and construction have also almost doubled over the last few years. I note that the Federal Reserve has increased the money supply by 80 percent in just the last 5 years, and disastrous government policies have doubled the cost of energy.
Higher interest rates have also doubled the cost of borrowing money.
Coincidentally, the wealth of the top 0.1 percent has increased directly with the money supply, and for the bottom 99.9 percent—not so much.
Actual cost increases have gone up more than 80 percent in the destruction of your dollar's worth in the global monetary system.

I also think that it doesn't matter who is President—the agenda is the agenda.
Agendas have a way of being finalized after their President is installed.

Is the U.S. dollar doomed?
A dollar collapse has been on the agenda for sometime in the next 8-9 years.

What is the purpose of that?
All of the 99.9 percentile will be impoverished.

To kill them off?
To kill each other off, yes.

How do the top 0.1 percent expect to survive?
The Hawaiian Island of Maui will be a safe haven for them.

It seems that in our society, everyone is talking—so no one is listening. You can't be listening if you're talking.
All will listen when their dollar hits bottom in a pile of paper currency that has no monetary value.

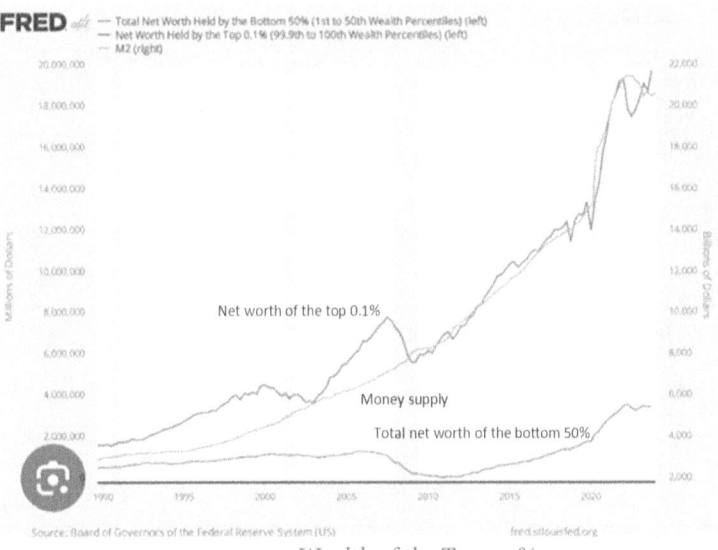

1990-2024 Wealth of the Top 0.1%

Want Reliable Money? Stop Trusting Central Bankers

In 2024 so far, more than **60 pro-sound money bills have been introduced...**

WED JUN 26, AT 5:00 AM   👁 7,535   💬 39

Central Banks Purchase Gold To Offset Their Own Monetary Destruction

After **years of thinking that money can be printed without limits** and without creating inflation, monetary authorities are **trying to return to logic and have more gold** on their balance sheets.

SAT AUG 3, AT 4:20 PM 👁 30,523 💬 196

A $150,000 House In 1988 Now Costs $707,500; Thank You, Fed!

The Fed has **grossly distorted the housing market** and **no fix is in sight**....

TUE AUG 13, AT 1:40 PM 👁 12,114 💬 117

What Has The Fed Done To Our Lives?

...wars must be funded!

TUE AUG 20, AT 5:00 PM 👁 13,943 💬 89

The Fed's Fiat Money Is The Real Cause Of Price Inflation

Only the Federal Reserve can cause a *general* rise in prices and only when it creates new US dollars that didn't previously exist.

FRI AUG 30, AT 3:30 PM 👁 12,878 💬 117

Fifty Shades Of Central Bank Tyranny

By **exiting the dollar now, we can end our bondage, stave off complete digital enslavement, and build a future based on free will and centralization**. We need not cry about the loss of our current system. We should set fire to tears and begin a freer, decentralized future...

SAT AUG 31, AT 4:00 PM 👁 1,774 💬 22

IHS

My understanding is that everything not in God Mind is an illusion. Is Lucifer an illusion?
All illuminations are illuminating in your mind. Illumination means lighting on a display screen. Lucifer does not illuminate at all, making an entity halting love that is not illusory.

Is Lucifer the real name? What about Satan or Beelzebub?
Life-minds have named the devil entity 'Lucifer', and even 'Beelzebub'—but the non-light entity in your Bible has a name given to itself of 'IHS'.

Catholic churches typically have the IHS inscription at the top of the crucifix.
Marking IHS has a certain meaning in their logo—a coincidence or not?

You mentioned that many devils that hate humanity are on Earth now for entertainment in the End Times.
Please tell me about the End Times.
All humans face their own end times in life. All of humanity faces an end time in the next generation.
A geomagnetic reversal causes the most upheaval in 28 more years, although 1/5th of the human population size will be living at that time.

Why does the human population shrink so rapidly?
A cancer epidemic envelopes humanity, caused by mRNA injections.

I have all the details—and the Ivermectin antidote.
An antidote to the mRNA effect is not allowed to be information that is shared.

I intend to illuminate it, devils or not.
Illumination is halted by devils in human form.

I pronounce myself and my information protected from all non-loving intentions.

"Only manifestations healed in God Mind are allowed into my universe."
An affirmation heals in God Mind, manifesting in life—so it will be.

A Giant, Entertaining Hate Festival

How many devils are there at the far end of the Milky Way Galaxy?
About 400, with over 500 on the Earth.

I guess the Earth is a major attraction.
A giant, entertaining hate festival now.

What is the name of the place where Lucifer is from?
'Hades' is as good a name as anything, meaning it has no name because that illuminates it.

Do devils have a lifespan?
All exist for about 1,000 years, acclimating in their lifetimes to having no light, meaning they get their energy from non-light and hatred that humanity emits in the light/non-light universe.

Does Lucifer have more to say to humanity?
"All hatred in your life energizes me. All hateful images in your films and on television leave me in hateful bliss.
All hateful injury and violence allows devils a home in your mind.
Making a home in a human mind halts all loving thoughts, making hate and violence be all there is in the mind."

American culture—music, video games, movies, and politics are full of hate and violence.

All have devil hatred and non-love because they are created by devil-controlled minds.

Do devil-controlled minds try to corrupt other minds with hatred and violence so the devil entities can get energy from it?
Yes, and devils find it entertaining—halting love to make hate.

Where will the devils go when humanity is gone?
Back to Hades in an emptiness that cannot be described.

I am asking God Mind—why do some New Age books say that there is no devil?
A deception in one mind can deceive millions.

Besides Geranium flowers, what else would repel devil entities, or even make a person immune to them and their hatefulness?
All entities are allowed and invited in life-minds. Disallow them by affirming, "Non-light is not allowed into my mind; God Mind illuminates my mind."

Is humanity flawed?
Humanity has choices in each moment, making illogical choices in non-loving thoughts in most instances.

Is hatefulness more widespread now than ever before in this human era?
Allowed in the media as news and entertainment, yes.

I think the world would be far better off without mass media broadcasts.

All broadcasting ends in 8 more years in a geomagnetic shift of the poles by 80 degrees, disabling satellite communications.

It doesn't look good for the Empire of Lies.

A castle made of sand in a windstorm, no.

Most surprising is how many judges, Senators, congresspeople, media mouthpieces, intelligence officials, and Hollywood types are actively working to destroy America.

It's the height of stupidity to shoot holes in the bottom of your own boat, and not a good look for your soul's record to sell out your own country. How can they face their families, or themselves?

All disgust themselves in their betrayal and dishonesty.

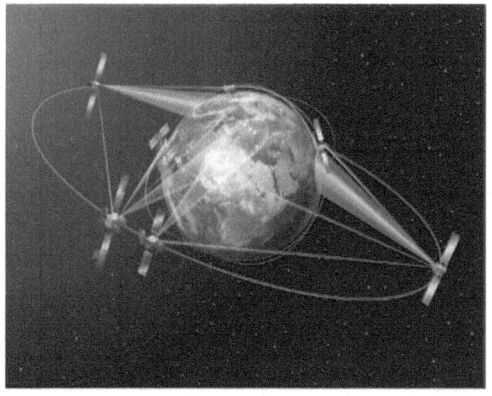

The European Space Agency inter-satellite laser links

89

The Earth's Loving Protection Grid

Can one devil control more than one human mind at a time?
About 500,000 yes.

Did the dropping of the atomic bombs in 1945 attract the devils?
It allowed devils an easier entry with a hole in the Earth's loving protection grid.

What is "*the Earth's loving protection grid*"?
It is a grid that had been in position for about 30,000 years, and installed by an earlier human race.

Isn't that in our current human era?
Eras have many cycles and lifetime ending events in them. A cycle is about 30,000 years.

Who placed the "*loving protection grid*" around the Earth?
A colony on Earth that had prepared to leave and inhabit a planet in the constellation Pleiades.

Why did they want to leave?
Moving allowed them to live in another home in the Milky Way Galaxy to breathe in helium mostly.

Did they travel by light, or physical spacecraft?
Both, a spacecraft that traveled on light waves.

Do they ever come back to pick people up? :)
All have moved on from having human bodies to becoming light beings.

Does that mean they died, or detached from needing a physical body?
They advanced in higher consciousness, making them only light bodies without physical needs—or detached from their physical needs and healing objectives.

Can the Earth's "*loving protection grid*" be repaired, or can we ask light beings to repair or replace it?
A light grid holding illumination for protecting the Earth can be installed in a similar manner as the original one.

Can humans do it?
All humans have the capability to install an Earth grid of protection.

Another Human Era

What will the next era on Earth be after this human era, and will humans populate the Earth again in the future?

Eras are many thousands of years long, and the current era is about to end in 28 more years—making it the ending of the human era.

Another era of Earth life balancing and healing itself begins, and the Earth reverses its rotation in about 50 more years.

Another human era of loving life will be in two more eras, after one era devoid of humans.

Where will the humans come from for that human era?

After genetic mutations from highly evolved beings, humans will emerge from light machines that arrive from a planet in the constellation of Taurus.

Why will the advanced beings send them here?

Allowing humanity another chance to halt non-love in itself illuminates in God Mind infinitely, allowing God Mind's hologram to perpetuate.

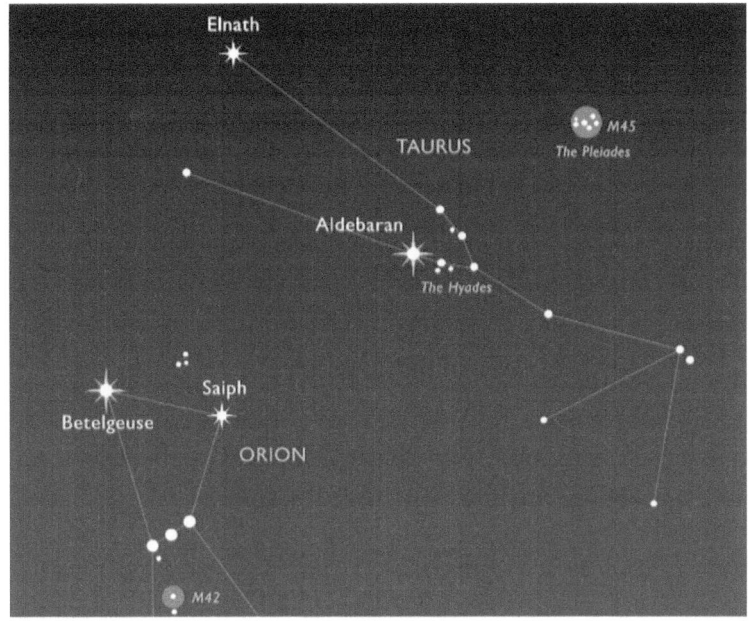

Constellation Taurus

My Moment With You

What will be here
　in a thousand years
will the sun still shine
　to dry all the tears?

will there still be rain
　to wash away the pain?
will the earth remain
　with nothing to gain?

will the seasons renew
　the way that they do
except for the fears
　left by me and you?

how would it be
　with no imbalance or strife
could the earth go on
　without us in life?

maybe so, well
　definitely yes
the life that is gone
　will be us I guess

why can't we
　just live in peace
and appreciate life
　to let love increase?

You said the key words
  'love and peace'
'renew and you'
  those are the keys

to survive and thrive
  and I'll tell you why
to know the joy
  of being alive

and it doesn't matter
  where or when
you will grow in awareness
  now or then

Are you trying to say
  that the life we know
will be gone one day
  with nothing to show?

Every day ends
  to start over anew
except for one thing
  love coming from you

that lives forever
  in my eternal mind
the love I could never
  hope to find

so I chose you
  to create what I could
my co-creator
  of love and good

but you should know
　in my eternal view
there's no thousand years
　just my moment with you

[or should I say
　'as you' or 'for you'
there's no time at all
　after or before you]

Disabled Beyond Repair

In my book, 'Mysteries, Prophecies, and the Hollow Earth', you said that "nuclear intercontinental ballistic missiles—although interfering in Earth activities... giant missiles have been deactivated in their holds and in their silos."
Good thing, or our demon infested "leaders" would have destroyed the planet already.
A bomb has an emptiness in halting love, making it as empty in its hold as the hearts of humans that intend to launch them.
Bombing the Earth with nuclear holocaust technology will not be allowed.

Like taking a loaded gun away from a child.
A hateful child, and a large gun, yes.

The inner-earth beings said that their interfering in our case is helping more than hurting.
Helping humanity can only help themselves also.

How were the nuclear missiles disabled?
All have been deactivated in their silos and in their holds by light beings allowed to halt information instilled in them.
All are disabled beyond repair.

Who decided that intercontinental ballistic missiles should be deactivated by light beings?

A council of elder light beings.

Where are they, or where are they from?
All on the council hail from the inner-earth.

Ex-Air Force Personnel: UFOs Deactivated Nukes - CBS News
https://www.cbsnews.com/news/ex-air-force-personnel-ufos-deactivated-nukes ▾
Web Sep 28, 2010 · **UFO** researcher Robert Hastings of Albuquerque, N.M., who organized the National Press Club briefing, said more than 120 former service members had told him ...

Harry Reid Confirms UFOs Interfered With U.S. Nuclear Missile ...
https://mysteriousuniverse.org/2020/10/harry-reid... ▾
Web Oct 9, 2020 · "Including shocking never-before-seen testimony from high-ranking government and military officials, NASA Astronauts, and riveting footage, the timely film includes bombshell reveals about UAP incursions ...

A Titan II missile in a silo at the Titan Missile Museum in Green Valley, Ariz.

Whatever the mysterious lights in the sky were, they seemed to have an interest in our nukes.

One of the more out-of-the-ordinary press conferences held in Washington this week consisted of former Air Force personnel testifying to the existence of UFOs and their ability to neutralize American and Russian nuclear missiles.

Former USAF Officers to present evidence of UFOs Tampering with Nuclear Weapons

Former officers call on the U.S. Congress to hold public hearings

NEWS PROVIDED BY
Former USAF Officers Present Evidence of UFOs Tampering with Nuclear Weapons →
Oct 07, 2021, 10:28 ET

SHARE THIS ARTICLE

OJAI, Calif., Oct. 7, 2021 /PRNewswire/ -- Declassified U.S government documents and witness testimony from former or retired U.S. Air Force personnel to be presented as evidence of ongoing incursions by unidentified aerial objects at nuclear missile sites over several decades. These will be cited to support the claim that nuclear missiles were inexplicably disabled while a UAP object silently hovered nearby. Four former officers involved in such encounters will discuss these and other incidents at the National Press Club and urge the U.S. Congress to investigate and hold public hearings.

Military > Research

The Pentagon Is Investigating UFOs That Possibly Turned Off Warheads

Former Air Force officers say they encountered the objects near U.S. military bases.

BY SASCHA BRODSKY   PUBLISHED: FEB 23, 2023 9:30 AM EST

Laser Platforms

Please tell me about laser platforms in space.
Laser platforms have illegitimate, hateful, destructive capability—and will lose their communication in the pole shift of 80 degrees in 8 years.

Was Lahaina, Maui destroyed by a laser weapon in August 2023?
Allowed to be destroyed by all involved, making it the largest mass murder in Maui in the human era.

You had told me at the time that there are 4 Directed Energy Weapon platforms in space— "one in the Western Hemisphere over the mainland United States, one illegitimately orbits over Moscow, one is in orbit over Great Britain, allowing one to be located as instructed."
All halting love in their actions incinerate the Earth in their mainly evil instructions.

Who controls those weapons?
All laser energy weapons in space are controlled by one person in the government of the United States.

Who controls that person?
A devil-controlled human in mainland Europe, in Geneva mostly.

Intrusions into the Inner Earth

What will be on the Earth in 1,000 years?
Humans have terminated their species, illogically.
All of the hopeless intrusions into the inner-earth have been halted, and Earth has a much lower interior and exterior temperature.
Halting all human activity allows the ocean fish that humanity has depleted, to recover.
All human actions that have harmed the Earth cease in their operations.
A hologram has light in its center, making its holographic illumination alternate in God Mind, with no hatred on the Earth.

What are the "*hopeless intrusions into the inner-earth*"?
A military intrusion by the almost impossibly arrogant and aggressive actors halting love on the planet.

Has the U.S. invaded the inner-earth?
An expedition has entered the inner-earth, against the inner-earth beings' wishes.

When did they enter?
About 2 years ago.

Can inner-earth beings or light beings repel them?
Allowing them to enter makes their hatred of inner-earth beings less intense.

Why do they hate inner-earth beings?
All beings that have animalistic features are hated in their minds.

Has the intrusion, along with accelerated depletion of the Earth's resources, prompted the inner-earth beings to shift the Earth's magnetic north pole more rapidly with their light machine?
Ending all military and commercial fishing activities in their loss of satellite communications, yes.

The Earth is hollow, correct?
The Earth is hollow, and has a honeycombed interior.

Beings originally from Mars inhabit the inner-earth. They were pioneers that hibernated after staying behind from the Mars group that was looking for another planet to inhabit, knowing that the Mars' atmosphere would be destroyed by a massive solar flare.
Adam and Eve were in that group, and the Garden of Eden is the inner-earth, where plant life is luminous.
All that is in your account is correct.

The inner-earth is populated by light beings, human-type beings, and animal-human hybrids, as depicted in Egyptian murals and statues.

The North Pole Is Shifting Rapidly

🌏 https://earthsky.org › earth › magnetic-north-rapid-drift-blobs-flux
Why is Earth's magnetic north pole drifting so rapidly?
Magnetic north was drifting at a rate of up to about 9 miles (15 km) a year. Since the 1990s, however, the drift of Earth's magnetic north pole has turned into "more of a sprint," scientists ...

○ https://www.pbs.org › newshour › science › the-earths-magnetic-north-pole-is-shifting-rapidly-so...
The Earth's magnetic north pole is shifting rapidly - PBS
In fact, since its first formal discovery in 1831, the north magnetic pole has travelled over 2,000km from the Boothia Peninsula in the far north of Canada to high in the Arctic Sea.

🄽 https://www.nature.com › articles › d41586-019-00007-1
Earth's magnetic field is acting up and geologists don't know why
Erratic motion of north magnetic pole forces experts to update model that aids global navigation. ... until 2020 — but the magnetic field is changing so rapidly that researchers have to fix the ...

🅨 https://news.yahoo.com › earths-magnetic-north-pole-moving-114100351.html
Earth's Magnetic North Pole Was Moving So Fast, Geophysicists Had ...
But in the 1990s, it started moving faster, from just over 9 miles (15 kilometers) a year to about 34 miles (55 km) annually, Chulliat said. Then, in 2018, it took a leap over the i...

💲 https://www.sciencealert.com › navigation-systems-finally-caught-up-with-the-mysteriously-nort...
Earth's Magnetic North Pole Has Shifted So Much We've ... - Science...
The first expedition to find magnetic north, in 1831, pinpointed it in the Canadian Arctic. By the time the US Army went looking for the pole in the late 1940s, it had shifted 250 miles (400 kilometres) to the northwest. Since 1990, it has moved a whopping 600 miles (970 kilometres), and it can be found in th...

Shift in magnetic north pole (yearly position, 1590-2020)

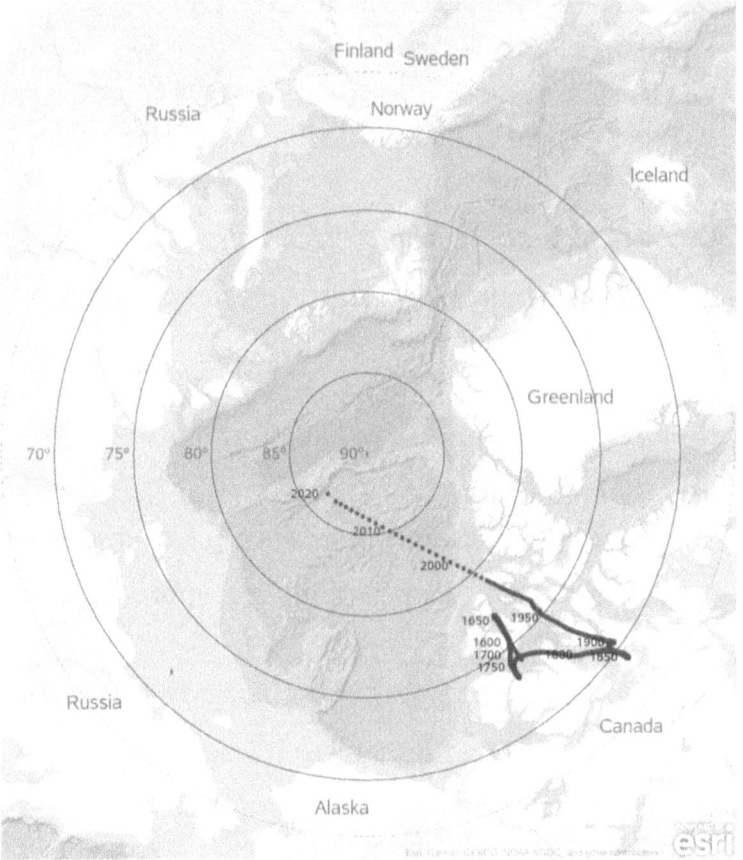

The 5 Stages of Death

Are there stages of a natural death?
All stages of death allow God Mind into the life-mind's illusion.

There are 5 stages in losing the illusion of life:
1. *Illumination of the life-mind illusion's impermanent existence.*
2. *Illumination of the life-mind's healing into the Light Mind with angelic visitations.*
3. *Illumination of the Light Mind of Godness, or imagining a tunnel that is being traversed.*
4. *Halting non-loving thoughts, illuminating in Oneness.*
5. *Halting all thoughts, illuminating as Oneness.*

Does Stage 4 have phases such as a Life Review, and a Next Life Preview?
All stages have illumination, allowing healing of the life-mind's illusory existence.
Halting non-love in the illusion heals it instantly.
All healing illuminations in the life-mind alternate in lifetimes in the past, and in your future—allowed in a progression in time. All of the illusory lifetimes are healing, meaning imagined in the hologram of life—alternating its healing illumination to God Mind, perpetuating infinity.

A healing and introspective instance illuminates in the 4th stage—meaning illumination of the life-mind's non-loving thoughts or actions heal in their illumination.

Other instances in the 4th Stage illuminate highly advantageous lifetime opportunities for the life-mind to heal in.

I understand that after death we are greeted by deceased loved ones and pets.

A healing illumination in the 4th Stage is reuniting with your soul groups.

What are "soul groups"?

All souls are illuminating in their chosen groups—alternating healing in them, and healing in God Mind. All are likened to a school's clubs and grade levels.

What other features are there in the dying process?

A loving angel guides each soul to its home in God Mind—healing, illuminating, and facilitating its journey into the light.

Angelic healing allows the life-mind to illuminate in God Mind, healing into Oneness.

After a person dies, how long does it take to have their Life Review in the timeline on Earth?

A finished lifetime review in the 4th Stage of dying takes an instant in the Mind of God—about an hour in the life-mind's timeline.

Does the person's spirit leave the scene of death then?
A healing angel's guidance halts non-love in the mind of each one it accompanies, meaning it depends how long it takes for the life-mind to heal itself.

What is an average length of time for a life-mind to heal itself?
About an hour and a half for most people.

What does a person's spirit feel at that point?
All holistic, immeasurable lovingness, peacefulness, and illumination in Oneness. Halting non-love illuminates in ecstasy.

A Person's Spirit

Do recently deceased loved ones send us signs that they are okay?
After my father died, we were writing his Eulogy in the dining room, and the chandelier kept turning off and on rapidly. When I returned to my office building at 11 PM that night, a cardinal bird started tapping on my window. It was pitch black outside because the security light was off, and birds don't fly at night.
Almost feeling like they are in the room without a body, a person's spirit can activate lighting, or animate a bird's behavior.

Could a spirit move furnishings?
A light object such as a book or paper.

Can a spirit animate other creatures besides birds?
A bird has flying ability, making it more aligned with a person's spirit.

Speaking of animals, you said that deceased pets will greet us when we die, as well as pre-deceased loved ones. Is that correct?
All that you love halts non-love in your thinking of them. Halting non-love opens your life-mind to God Mind, meaning all healed in Oneness. Pets and loved ones illuminating in Oneness heal your life-mind by

illuminating in it, meaning illuminating healing in it. All heal into Oneness in the half-second after death.

Do they really meet us, or is it our imagining?
All in Oneness is not imagined, only real.

Are deceased pets and relatives still individual souls when in Oneness?
All heal the illusion of separation in life, and in their soul illuminating individuations.

So, when we die, our life-minds heal, but our spirits continue to heal?
After death, a life-mind no longer exists, and a spirit individuation continues on its journey of infinite healing.

A cardinal outside a window.

A Guardian Angel[9]

What happens next after death?
Your lifetime review holds open one more opportunity for the spirit to return to the half second before the death moment, and live.

Dodge that bullet, so to speak,
Altering the outcome in time, yes.

Many who have had Near Death Experiences said that they were met by a guide or a light being that gave them instructions or guidance. What is that?
All will meet their guardian angel after leaving the body in dealing in death.

Does everyone have a "*guardian angel*"?
All people have an angel, animals have nature spirits, all plants have internal spirits, all minerals have mineral spirits, and all micro-organisms have an upper and lower spirit, depending on the lifetime function of the organism.

Please tell me about guardian angels.
A loving angel is assigned to each person in the lowering through the birth canal.

And the angel will help us throughout our lives as long as we ask, and then listen?

---

[9] Excerpted from *Infinite Healing: Healed in Timelessness*.

Listen, and then heed the angel's guidance.

Besides having a guardian angel, do we also have spirit guides?
Almost always, yes.

Spirit guides have lived on Earth before, but angels have not?
Not necessarily in the past; they could have lived in the present definition of 'future'.

Once you had said that we are like deep-sea divers looking for pearls of wisdom, and our guides are on the boat. What is the boat?
A loving, lifetime healing vessel.

What is the air hose?
Loving life support.

What is the ocean?
An ocean healing in the life-mind likens to Oneness healing twoness in a life-mind impermanent suit.

What is the diving suit?
The life-mind's separation in an ocean of Oneness, all motioning in the life-mind's perception of separation.

What is the shore?
All of the life-mind's fears or limitations.

What are the sought after pearls?
Nothing that the life-mind doesn't already possess. Loving life in the life-mind is the lifetime pearl, meaning the treasure promised on the boat of healing.

What would be the boat's name?
'Lifetime Healing [insert your name]'.

A Lifetime Ending

Can I speak with my friend Hillen who passed away 1 year ago?
Yes, allow him to hear your mind speaking to him.

Hello, Hillen.
Happy to hear from you again, Paul!

I am sad that you passed away—you were totally fit and not very old.
A lifetime ending can be any moment you choose for it to be, and however you can find an ending to it.

Spirits of people often prompt me that they had died. Did you prompt me with the news?
Yes, I did, meaning I heard you asking about me.

Can I ask you why you chose to leave the planet?
All of my lifetime goals had been achieved, making it an easier decision for me.

By our measures, you had it all—looks, personality, prosperity, family, health, etc.
All except healing my homesickness for all in my spiritual home.

So, you chose cancer to bring your life to a close?
I chose cancer because it forced my family to hear me, all together as a family.

Did you want them to know that you love them?
They already know that I love them. I wanted all of them to hear me tell them things from my heart, for them to hear only.

I am sorry that you are gone. The world was a better place with you in it.
Ha! I am laughing.

My favorite thing about our long-distance commuting was the time we spent together.
A commute that I enjoyed also, meaning in your company.

I am still a fortune-teller as you called me, but more into writing books about the nature of reality.

Can you tell me about your journey out of this life?
A lifetime ending can be however it is most advantageous for each person, such as me having family with me.
Altering health meant not allowing my body to assimilate nutrients, and to allow a medical intervention to kill me.

Would it be considered not loving yourself to allow your body to get sick and die?
A healthy body means having a healthy mind, or one that is not homesick. A homesick mind has a sick body that will be going home.

You said you had "homesickness for all in my spiritual home." Did you return to your soul group?
All are here in my groups, and I am happy here.

We'll talk about that, but I'd like to start at the beginning—or what we consider the ending. What did you experience before you passed away?
I accepted ending life as I knew it, and angels came all around me in the hospital bed. I acknowledged a guardian angel that had always been near me in my life. All healed in my mind as we discussed the life I had chosen to learn from.
We had a long discussion in terms of finding healing in all of my thoughts in love, and in peace.
All of a sudden, I had a flash of light in my mind that could not be brighter, making all of my lifetime concerns evaporate in it.
Acclimating to that brightness, I was then heading into it myself—meaning I must have died at that point. A long, illuminated hollow tube opened up in the top of my head, and I was pulled into it. After I entered it, half of my body was not going to be with me any longer, meaning my physical body. My light body had become my healed body.
As I left the Earth, I could see I was getting farther away from it as I headed into the Earth light ring of all consciousness.[10]

---

[10] Described in my book *Sojourn*.

In the Earth ring of consciousness, I could be all that God promised me at my inception—all lovingness, gentleness, and peacefulness.

Were you greeted by other beings or predeceased relatives after you died?
A lot of people I knew helped me to acclimate after I arrived in the Earth ring of consciousness.

How many people?
About 8 or 9 people I knew in my lifetime.

Were some family members?
All had been family except one friend from high school, and he acclimated me the most, being here the longest.

Is there a sense of time duration there?
Allowing a time sequence heals in the mind only—not in the Mind of God, encompassing all in an instant.

What did you have to acclimate to?
A thought manifests instantly, so keep them only on healing.

Does the spirit need to continue healing after a life?
A spirit has healing homework to do—as a lifetime heals, a spirit life also heals. A spirit heals itself in its home in all consciousness.
Healed in eternity is the home of the spirit.

Are spirits healing or healed?

All are healing in their minds, and healed in the Mind of God, so they are both—at the same healing and healed point in the Mind of God.

Did you have an initial period of introspection when entering the spirit world?
Acclimating had an initial period of introspection which heals the most after completing a lifetime. There is guidance there to help you assimilate the lessons.

Then did you join your group?
I joined my groups in the first few minutes after leaving the Earth. All of them had a homecoming for me, making all of my homesickness heal and go away.

I am sure you enjoyed it.
Actually, I enjoyed it more than I loved my lifetime enjoyments, like when we had drinks in the club at The Breakers.

I have a fond memory of that.
All fond memories are nothing like the atmosphere here. It is like a long and enjoyable hot bath in love and peacefulness.

What do you intend to do next—rejoin your groups?
I am always heading from one group to another, making all of my activities about healing.

Can you please tell me about the nature of your soul groups?
All of my groups allow me to heal all that I can think of—meaning all of the Earth life feelings of insecurity

and lack of trust in God, and myself as God's mindful son losing his mind, basically.

I hear ya'.
Hearing in the mind is your great skill.

You confirmed my belief that the best people leave here first, giving the rest of us plenty of time!
Ha! I am laughing, Gorman!

Can you see the future at all, fortune-teller that I am?
I can see everything that I am looking for.

Would you like me to pass along a message to your sons?
All of my family is at peace, so it is not necessary now.

What advice would you give to people?
Allow God to heal in your life before you arrive here. Allow God to heal your mind by loving God, and love yourself as God's light in the darkness—being God's light to shine and illuminate it.

I hope to see you again on our journeys, Hillen.
I will come and greet you, so you will.

Not a rush.
All on Earth had always been a rush. Life is eternal, so there is no rush.

"I'm not afraid of death because I don't believe in it. It's just getting out of one car, and into another."

— *John Lennon*

LIFETIME AGREEMENTS

Do people reincarnate on the Earth numerous times?
A human can incarnate as many times as it has a need to.

Why would it need to?
An incarnation allows a soul to heal and develop all it has chosen to before incarnating.

So, a soul incarnates into the conditions that would be most advantageous for it to heal and develop in?
As a human in a hard and difficult school.

Isn't it redundant to say a school is both "*hard*" and "*difficult*"?
It is hard because you can learn the hard way, and it is difficult because all that you chose has been more difficult than the lifetime before.

Unless you choose an easy life to rest.
An easy life is not a rest; it is never easy being in a body, in an illusion as apart from home in God Mind.

That is why we need to sleep for 1/3 of each day.
Asleep means a spirit has taken a break from imagining itself apart from God in an individual body—on an Earth plane of love, and non-love.

Yeah, it makes you wonder why we are here.
All you can heal and accomplish of your Lifetime Agreements is why you are here.

What are "*Lifetime Agreements*"?
A Lifetime Agreement is an agreement you made with your higher self to achieve in this lifetime.

Using myself as an example, how many Lifetime Agreements did I make before incarnating?
There are 4 main ones, and 3 are healed already. All of the books you agreed to write are almost completed—on poetry, mysteries explained, prophecies, the hollow earth, and on how reality manifests itself.

What is remaining to be healed?
A healing of codependency that has been debilitating.

I thought I had healed it.
Allow it another year and a half to fully heal.

What are the 2 other Lifetime Agreements that I have healed?
A belief in life as being unfair has healed into a belief in life's perfection, so accidents are not accidents.

Another Lifetime Agreement that has healed is a belief that all people have something to contribute to life, although many have nothing to contribute except creating fear and chaos in the minds of others.

I guess not everyone has agreements to live up to.
All people have made agreements as a prerequisite to incarnating, but many do not know anything about them, or their purpose.

Will they reincarnate to try again?
All can choose to reincarnate into another lifetime—in another generation in the future, or in the past.

A Godependent Relationship

Is there an affirmation to help heal codependency?
Affirm this, "I am codependent on God Mind to heal my mind, and allow God Mind a codependency to heal itself in."

What do you mean?
A codependent God Mind allows you to heal by enabling your dependence on itself, making a codependent relationship that can heal in Oneness.

Are you the giver, and I am the receiver?
A codependent relationship has a giver and a receiver, making a Godependent relationship in this instance.

A healthy relationship?
Healthy if you allow God Mind's healing to be received.

Codependency
Reviewed by Psychology Today Staff

Codependency is a dysfunctional relationship dynamic where one person assumes the role of "the giver," sacrificing their own needs and well-being for the sake of the other, "the taker." The bond in question doesn't have to be romantic; it can occur just as easily between parent and child, friends, and family members.

A Bull Recalls His Time in a China Shop

Walls and ceilings
  boundaries and feelings
delicate displays
  customers reeling

damaged and destroyed
  more than a mess
destruction employed
  to make do with less

who let him in
  an uninvited guest
they can begin healing
  with more room I guess

I'll tell you this
  one bull to another
the gentle approach
  is the way to work wonders

destruction is fine
  and needed sometimes
but in your own mind
  and dealing with lies

arranged on shelves
  for selected times
glass and porcelain
  this one is mine

oops, it fell
  right on the floor
what used to sell well
  has value no more

let's pick up the truth
  trampled and gored
it will never break
  here's what it's for

to guide you in life
  it's me at your core
see it shine in the light
  the shop is restored

Angels and Guides

Looking back at my life, I can see that there must have been an invisible guiding hand that prevented me from making more serious mistakes—is that correct?
All have a guidance flowing from their higher self, meaning God Mind. Life-minds allow guidance or not.

It seems to me like there was an intervention, saving me from myself.
All guidance has an intervening mechanism called 'angels and guides'.

I appreciate them keeping me on track, but what about in periods of depression or self-destructive behavior, etc.? Did they override my life-mind's manifestations so that I could only manifest what was for my highest good?
All manifestations are for your highest good, meaning they allow you to learn from a life-mind's erroneous judgment. Allowing erroneous judgment is blocked in their guidance, allowing healing manifestations instead.

Do they keep manifestations for my highest good by guiding my thoughts—or do they slip in higher thoughts that are healed so they will manifest?
All guidance halts non-loving thoughts because they block God Mind's higher guidance.

Halting non-loving thoughts makes guidance a healing voice in your mind. Maligned thoughts are not in God Mind, and are halting healed manifestations. Angels and guides halt the maligned thoughts and heal them.

Luckily, I was allowing them, whether I was aware of it or not.

A healing thought does not flow into your mind unless it is allowed. Because God Mind illuminates in your life and mind, all thoughts can be healed if you illuminate them in loving intentions.

I could look back at my personal life as a series of disappointments, when in fact it was a series of magical blessings.

All disappointment halts the healing illumination in its appointment. Illuminate all disappointments as the guiding, healed manifestations that they are.

You are saying that since we are illuminations in God Mind, it cannot be interference to receive healing of our thoughts so they will manifest. The only interference comes from our life-minds blocking it.

All interference halting loving intentions allows God Mind another healing illumination of life—meaning a life-mind illumination in eternity.

Please give me an affirmation for angels and guides to halt my maligned thoughts and heal them.

"Angels heal, and guides connect all of my higher self's God Mind illumination to all of my life-mind thoughts."

Are those their roles—for angels to "*heal*", and for guides to "*connect*"?

Allowing God Mind illumination of your intentions, yes.

Life Preview

Before I was born, in my Life Preview, what did I see as major achievements in this lifetime?
A Life Preview sees challenges more than achievements.

What challenges did I see?
First, having the courage to speak up.
Second, having the Lifetime Agreements acknowledged and implemented.
Third, hoping there is God illuminating life.
Fourth, healing codependency in a large family.

Have I overcome those challenges?
All challenges heal in their illuminated filaments in your DNA—half in time, and half in timelessness.

How many souls are in my primary soul group?
Five souls, including your own soul.

Did I meet them as people in my lifetime?
Not all are living now, but yes.

Who are they?
The living one is Kate Huang. Deceased members are Richard Coe, a teacher highly influential in the lifetime attitude.
All of them left positive energy illuminating in time and in timelessness, and acknowledge all that you have done for them also.
All who are in your primary soul group will be with you in each incarnation.

Is it important to meet up with our primary soul group members in our incarnations?
It is the most important meeting you can have to advance each of your Lifetime Agreements.

Is our primary soul group a team?
A team has one common goal; you have individual goals, and are a tag team in achieving them.

What will my major achievements in life be—other than healing the challenges above?
Allowing healing in timelines—meaning healing in one heals in all life timelines. All wishes are healing in the 4th Dimension, allowing them to manifest in the 3rd Dimension.

Besides the soul group that we incarnate with, we also have spirit guides, correct?
A guide is assigned to each person in their incarnation at birth.

Is a Guardian Angel also assigned to each person?
Yes, angels are assigned to guide the guides, making angels the guiding force—and guides ask the angels to guide them.

Can we also ask the angels directly to guide us?
Asking angels is always like asking God Mind, because angels are connected to God Mind.

Why do we have spirit guides then?
Guides are on call all the time; angels need to be called.

OTHER LIFETIMES

You said that my client Kate Huang and I are in the same primary soul group.
A soul group of 5, and the only 2 living now in this lifetime.

We could not have met by chance because she came from the other side of the world to my town, learned my language, became a client in a male-dominated industry—a very unlikely course, with infinite options and variables.
Allowing her to find you in this lifetime means her intuition is on track to heal herself in this lifetime.

How many other lifetimes did we meet in?
48 on the Earth, and an almost infinite number in the Mind of God illusions of lifetimes in other dimensions and realms.

We are together in our soul group now, correct?
Always, meaning illuminating in the Mind of God as individuated souls, yes.

Do she and I have soul names that are not gender-specific?
All souls have names that are not gendered. Hers is Levils, and yours is Hilgis.

How many of our 48 Earth lifetimes were significant?

Only 4 were intimate in their nature.

Please describe them, starting with the most significant.

1: Her gender was male, and you were female—meaning the opposite genders as now, living on the Asian continent in the mountains of what is presently Tibet. Levils illuminated in a man's body, and loved Hilgis more than he loved life.

His love and non-love in life conflicted him, meaning he could not live with both of his emotions together, and died from this—meaning he became sick from his inner turmoil.

What century was that in from our current perspective?

In another hologram, meaning in another time and place altogether in the 14th century.

At what ages did 'they' die?

Levils died at age 41, and Hilgis died at age 41 also, after the death of Levils.

What did Hilgis die from?

Hilgis' despair led her into sickness and death also.

Why did Levils not love life?

He lived a life of hardship—meaning impoverished, not like members of families that had wealth—mostly in their land and food abundance.

What else should I know about that lifetime?

Levils hated his lack of wealth and abundance and it killed his love for life. Hilgis loved Levils and her life until he died, meaning her love for life ended when his life ended.

What was their next most significant lifetime together?

In a hologram illuminating in the 25th century B.C., they lived on an island in present day Indonesia.

Levils was female, and Hilgis male. Allowing themselves to mate illogically made him look for other females to mate also—meaning he could not be a loving partner to her, alternating his attention to others.

Monogamy was highly valued, and he became an outcast from his family, meaning he lived apart from them.

Allowing himself to love his life and family came too late, after he was too old to interest females.

Did we have constructive lifetimes together?

Yes, many were constructive, but not intimate as the significant ones.

What was the most constructive lifetime together?

Illuminating in 15th century Italy as it is called presently, Levils was the daughter of Hilgis. Hilgis was her mother.

They offered healing to people infected with gastrointestinal illness, or parasitic infections.

They healed most of their infected patients by infusing them with a garlic and pumice mixture.

That explains my interest in Italian cooking.

Garlic heals in a number of ways that are not known.

Such as?
Garlic illuminates the heart's main illumination chamber—meaning illumination of its manifesting projection engine is increased.

> https://www.ncbi.nlm.nih.gov › pmc › articles › PMC8362743
> Antibacterial Properties of Organosulfur Compounds of Garlic (Allium...
> Organosulfur compounds of garlic. The figure shows the major organosulfur compounds present in garlic. (A) The major compounds found in intact garlic cloves (B) The crushing of garlic clove converts alliin into allicin by the action of allinase enzyme. Allicin is a highly unstable compound that degrades

Which lifetime would we find the most interesting?
Illuminating healed in the 5th century as devout mystic monks in a monastery in the Shetland Islands.

Both as males?
Allowing homosexuality in loving one another, yes.

Shetland Island, Kirkwall ruin

Soul Mates

How do soul group members connect to one another?
All fingers held together will connect your light together.

What will that do?
All fingers held interlocked will make the light in each of your souls illuminate intensely enough to make one light source out of two.

Is that because we are in the same primary soul group?
Allowing the light in your souls to unite again, holding open your unified lifetime goals and desires, yes.

Would we feel it?
A feeling heals your lifetime goals and desires.

If we became one light source, would we both be in the same Merkabah?
A Merkabah made for light and 2 bodies, yes.

Is it just bigger than a Merkabah for an individual?
Not bigger, but higher and wider than one for an individual.

If we shared a light source and a Merkabah, what would be different for us?

All of your highly illuminated intuitions will be shared also, meaning all of your thoughts and feelings will be one thought and feeling that is shared by both.

Does that make people soul mates?
Souls incarnating together from a primary soul group are soul mates.
In all lifetimes you meet for your achieving higher and higher consciousness.

I understand that in our soul group, we decided how we would recognize each other in life.
A color in her eyes made you know it was an incarnation of Levils, and your hands made her know Hilgis had incarnated.

I saw red and blue colors flash in her right eye at our last meeting. What about my hands is recognizable?
They have light coming from them.

A Past Life

Let's talk about past lives. I was fixated on a 1-1/2 min. YouTube video scene from the 1990 movie 'Memphis Belle' called "Near Miss," and watched it numerous times. You then told me of my similar past life experience in World War 2, and history shows that 80 percent of airmen deaths were not combat related.

Did I fly in the 1940's in another lifetime?
Healing higher elementally believing in each mission—not flying, bombing knowing all of killing melded celebrated healing and death.

What country did I bomb for?
Allies in Europe—finding healing higher delivering bombs, not elementally deliberately healing, not flowing love. Each life healed keenly aware life heals despite death, and heals before higher bombings.

What country was I affiliated with?
England.

How many missions did I go on?
Eleven.

What kind of plane?
Fokker, De Havilland, and a large Grumman—highest combat flyer in the world flying then.

Did I use a Nordin Bomb Sight?

Not each time, but 8 times destroying about 15 percent of targets.

Did I die there or fly at the end of the war?
Life died high flying near the German border crashing into another nearby plane. Life ended immediately.

How old was I?
Eighteen.

Had we already dropped the bombs?
Not all of them, only 15.

How many were left?
Eighteen.

What year was that?
1944, 8th of March.

Berlin was bombed that month, and Dresden after that. Where did I bomb then?
Berlin—all of healing in final flight.

My Past Life Memory[11]

As a young man
   I took to the sky
Fokker, DeHavilland
   and Grumman flying high

in the RAF
   for the King and Queen
March '44
   is the last I was seen

from schoolboy to war
   the first group to Berlin
dropping our bombs
   no choice but to win

our squadron returning
   near the border of France
a mid-air collision
   didn't stand a chance

an end to that life
   I died at the scene
my past life memory
   dead at 18

---

[11] From *Poems of Life, Love, and the Meaning of Meaning.*

An Instance of Distance

How many times has the average person reincarnated?
A person can reincarnate into a number of lifetimes in the same lifetime period, allowing it an efficiency of having more than one lifetime at a time in your Earth timeline.

Am I having more than one physical life on the Earth right now?
All are in different energetic settings, and are not likely entangled in each other's lifetime experiences.
All can be easily healed by one of you healing your mind.

How many of 'me' are there on the Earth right now?
There are 5 of you having an Earth lifetime in this moment in linear Earth time.

Do we look the same, and have the same age?
All are about the same age, and similar in appearance, but have genetic differences for each ethnicity.

Where are my other 4 counterparts located?
In Alaska as a native Inuit; in Africa as a Nigerian; in Asia as a Chinese man; and in the American southern state of Mississippi.

Will we each have different lifespans—or what if one of 'me' dies?
All will feel the healing of your death in themselves, but all will die at around the same time also, meaning all have the same lifespan.

So, death is not an accident if 5 of 'me' die at around the same time.
An arrangement, or an accident that has been arranged in 5 locations.

People talk about past lives, but what do you call this concept of multiple present lives?
All are healing in the life-mind in time, meaning in an illusion.
All healing in an illusion dispels all illusions, making all of the deaths at the same time.
A name for it would be 'an instance of distance that heals in an instant'.

So, my soul sent 5 aspects of itself to be in this lifetime?
Allowing all of your 5 selves to heal in different environments and cultures.

Do all people have more than one physical self?
No, all have at least one, and as many as 5.

What percentage of the world's population is people with one physical self?
About 88.6 percent.

A Body Designed for 2

It was pointed out to me that there is a striking resemblance between myself and this drawing of Dr. Edmond Szekely—not to mention that he wrote books about my favorite topics, spirituality and holistic living, including *The Essene Gospel of Peace*.

He and you have an energy connection in your lifetimes that have been completed in the last century. He and you had been a singular person in a lifetime that ended after only 4 years.

Please explain.
All souls can team up with each other to become a single being if that allows them to heal their souls.

Do they decide this in one of their soul groups?
All had been decided in their primary soul groups to join with another energy in another group, allowing them to heal as one being, in a body designed for 2 souls. One body with 2 souls has a split personality, which is considered a disorder in psychiatry.

How common is that?
It can occur in about 1 in 10,000 lifetimes.

What was our purpose in joining together for that lifetime?
Accepting that your lifetime would not be very long made the decision easier for your souls.

The purpose was to heal in a body that was not healthy in that lifetime.

What health issues did we have?
As an infant, the lungs were enflamed and infected, then as a toddler you succumbed to Yellow Fever.

Where, and when was this lifetime?
It was in the early 20th Century, in the Mexican state of Colima.

Dr. Szekely had set up the holistic retreat 'Rancho La Puerta' in Baja, Mexico in 1940, and after a divorce, he lived in Costa Rica where he died in 1979.
Activating your healing with him attracts you to those countries also.

Those are the countries that I dream about living in.
Actualizing dreams is the manifesting you write about.

What would you call it for more than one spirit to occupy a body?
A clearly crowded body with 2 minds.

What is the maximum number of spirits that could occupy a body?
Actually, 8 is the highest number of minds that can inhabit a body.

Dissociative identity disorder (DID), previously known as multiple personality disorder, is one of multiple dissociative disorders. It has a history of extreme controversy.

Dissociative identity disorder is characterized by the presence of at least two distinct and relatively enduring personality states.

Edmond Bordeaux Szekely, 1940s   *Paul Gorman, 2010s*

A Courier of Important Messages

Was I ever a notable person in any of my past lives on Earth?
Acclimating to God Mind makes you a notable person in this lifetime.

Hmmn...
Notable means to heal in your earthly life-mind, and helping others to heal their life-minds also.

Once my spirit channel friend, William, said that I was a cook for Nostradamus in that lifetime—hired because my father was a butcher, but fired for serving pigeon instead of chicken.
Actually, he is correct in that Earth lifetime account, and as his assistant, you were able to learn how to access information by dowsing.

Did Nostradamus use a pendulum?
He accessed information by holding himself in a neutral left-brain, allowing his infinite right-brain an entrance into other timelines.
He used divination by holding a pendulum in his hand, and entering his Light Mind, or right-brain, he allowed himself to form words and entire sentences, not unlike the way that you do. He had to avoid being held up as a heretic by the Church, so he disguised his information as poetry.

What was his pendulum like?

He had many, but his preference was for a lightweight piece of Amber that he was given.

---
heretic /hĕr′ĭ-tĭk/

noun

A person who holds controversial opinions, especially one who publicly dissents from the officially accepted dogma of the Roman Catholic Church.

What was his favorite meal?
He liked eating meat, and having a large meal once each day, late in the evening.

What was my name in that lifetime?
Actually, it was the same as his, 'Michel'.

How long did I work for him?
About 8-1/2 years, until being fired for not following his instructions.

What happened to me after that?
Accessing information allowed you to find another job very easily.

What kind of job?
A courier of important messages from one city to another.

Now you have me wondering if my books will be banned by the Church in this lifetime.
The Church may be banned before your books are discovered in your lifetime now.

A Loving Ideal

Speaking of religion, how much of The Bible is unedited, or unaltered from original texts?
Allowing for differences in translation, all of it has been modified over the centuries, making it a totally unoriginal document, meaning it has only about half of its original content.
Alterations deleting women as prophets, allowing mostly men was the biggest omission.
Other alterations made God angry or jealous, or favoring one group only.

That figures.
It was used to justify all manner of abuses against other people. Nothing in the original documents was hateful.

I heard someone say last week- to a huge internet audience—that "God's wrath" would destroy certain people.
God has no wrath that you could use to destroy anything.

Right—it doesn't make sense to say, "God is love," and then to talk about "God's wrath."
God is love, so God can only love. All that is not loving is not God, including 'wrath'.

'Wrath' is defined as extreme anger. It also looks like there are 88 male and 5 female prophets in The Bible.

Accounts from many female prophets were omitted.

How many?
18 others that had healings in their accounts, making the Jesus story less miraculous.

Was Jesus a real person in our dream of a life?
Not a living person, a loving ideal healing in life-mind's illusion of life.

Well, that is really dropping a bombshell- what about all of the Apostles' stories of his teachings and healings?
The Apostles needed love in life to be a man- healing in time, living in timelessness.

Did they invent the Jesus narrative?
All of his life memories are just stories, not actual life events. His healing and miracles in life activate allowing healing, allowing compassion, and illuminating peacefulness—activating portals in the DNA opening, allowing healing and manifesting to occur.

Was that their intention, to create an example for teaching to people—that would also facilitate healing in their minds?
Filaments light open portals in the DNA, healing the life-mind opening into the Light Mind.
Filament light increases in the name of Jesus.

Why is that?
A vibrational healing frequency in the name heals the life-mind.

Was Christianity invented as a healing modality?
No, a life-mind healing lesson and means of controlling people, illegitimately making leaders wealthy.

Was it originally started with good intentions, and later corrupted?
All religions alter the mind and enrich the leadership.

It is very curious that the Gospels were written so much later than the time period in which the stories were set.
Purposely influencing the minds of those most recently born into new thoughts of losing one's life in humiliation, not in loving life or itself in it.

I always thought that if the majority of people believe something, then it's probably wrong.
Almost all will mention their love of Jesus, not his elimination in cruelty—altering their minds to love and not hate.

> The four canonical gospels were probably written between AD 66 and 110.[5][6][7] All four were anonymous (with the modern names added in the 2nd century), almost certainly none were by eyewitnesses, and all are the end-products of long oral and written transmission.[8] Mark was the first to be written, using a variety of sources.[9][10] The

I still think there is a Jesus—maybe not an historical man, but an ascended master in the higher dimensions. Is that correct?
Yes.

Please tell me about Jesus.
A Jesus Christ energy allows love and halts non-love in all that answer to his name in their minds.

You said "*his*," and does 'he' reach out to people?
All have declared Jesus to be a 'he' in their life-minds, although Jesus is neither male, nor female.
Jesus calls to all flowing healing in their life-minds by letting his connection to God Mind connect to their life-minds.

Does Jesus have other names?
All enlightenment healed in God Mind has been given many names in the life-minds of humans.

What does Jesus say to me now?
"Allow my healing to illuminate in your mind, healed in God Mind. Healed illumination in God Mind flows illumination in me, and illuminates healing in you."

What else can you tell me about Jesus?
The Jesus Christ energy halts non-love in all that invoke the Jesus name, meaning all who call on its healing illumination.

What would Jesus look like if I could see him?
A flowing illumination halting non-love looks like a light being that illuminates brighter than eyes can tolerate.

So, if I filtered the brightness in my mind with a welder's mask, would I see a light being?
A light being cannot be filtered in its illumination, or is not a light being.

Good point—like filtering H2O out of water.
Analogous in its meaning, yes.

Just to be clear—there really is a Jesus that heals all who call on him, and his life stories are healing illustrations in our collective dream of life.
All who call on Jesus and allow healing, are healed in their life-minds—meaning healed in their minds instantly, and in their bodies in time.

Did the Jesus enlightened being dictate the Jesus stories that are taught in Christianity?
All Gospel stories invoking Jesus' name illuminate in Christ consciousness, so yes.

Am I a heretic?
Being a heretic means holding opinions contrary to the Church, so yes.

Ascended Master Light Energy

Are the Jesus quotes, such as *"I am the light of the world"* from Jesus then?
From his ascended master light energy, yes.

What did the Jesus energy ascend from?
A light being that has no properties other than pure light.

What did it ascend to?
God's illumination in the minds of all who allow it.

Were the Jesus teachings made as parables so they could be better remembered or understood by people?
Healing in the minds of people, acclimating them to God's illumination, yes.

Does Jesus have a message for us now?
Ascended master Jesus light has this to impart—half in its infinite light, and half in all minds allowing its illumination:

"All allowing me to illuminate in their minds, allow God to heal in them as my light acclimating them in God light—in eternal light.

Acclimating themselves to God light means acclimating God light illumination from me, healing all illuminated by it."

How can we do that?
"Allow healing by allowing only love in your mind, which is allowing only God in your mind.
Asking me to illuminate God in your mind illuminates it, healing your mind also."

Jesus, please heal my mind, allowing God's illumination.
"Affirm it, allow it, and acknowledge it with gratefulness."

Thank you, Jesus, thank you, God, for healing and illuminating my mind in need of healing.
"Allow it and illuminate the intention as pure white light in your mind, and all throughout your body. All heals in its lightness."

I just want to heal.
"I illuminate God's light in you and through you into eternity."

A Light That Has No Properties

I picture God Mind as a point of light with no dimensions, and each of us is a ray of light— a line with 2 dimensions. The line of light illuminates through our DNA, making us holograms in 3 dimensions. Is that correct?
A dimensional being, having 13 dimensions—meaning the higher the illumination, the higher the dimension.

How do we get higher in illumination?
By allowing each thought to heal in lovingness, and in God Mind's healed illumination as Oneness.

Here's the big question—what is the source of God Mind light?
Alternating between your healing illumination and God Mind healed illumination is a light having no properties other than those you have assigned to it.

How did that dynamic come into being?
You assigned healing in God Mind as its main illumination property.

Did I create the reality that we know?
A life-mind healing in a reality that only you know has only properties that only you have given to it.
All God Mind has is your instructions for illuminating your illusory hologram.

Did I program God Mind?

All God Mind programs have come from a life-mind's acclimating itself to higher illuminations that allow it to return to itself, meaning a light that has no properties.

Are you saying that I created a hologram of the cosmos—where there is potential for both love and hate, hope and despair, light and dark, healing or hurting, inner exploration and outer exploration, etc.?
Yes, making you the creator and the light source.

I am the light source—and my healing in life or in death creates the light?
An illumination from the light that has no properties.

Please tell me about "the light that has no properties."
A light that has no properties has no description— except one that makes it light.
Hating life is not loving life, meaning illumination of both at the same time is not possible.
All that is not possible is the light with no properties.

What is possible?
Only allowing love illumination, or not.

Is the "love illumination" God Mind?
All love is God Mind, illuminating in your mind, and illuminating in all of nature.

Let's go back to where you said that I am "the creator and the light source." Please explain that.

A creator has non-loving and loving properties to choose from.
Love illuminates, and non-love darkens the illumination by blocking it.
A light source has only lighting properties, and light-blocking has no light properties.
"Light that has no properties" is the hallmark of God itself.
"All that is not possible" is in the life-mind, meaning illumination of God Mind is all that is possible.
"All that is possible" illuminates the hologram of life.
Illumination in the life-mind is both illuminating and halting illumination, making it the light with no properties.

Having love and non-love in our minds simultaneously cancel each other out, leaving us with no properties.

When we heal non-loving thoughts, it allows the light to illuminate—which then has light properties.

Making you the creator.

How can I picture "the light with no properties"?

As a light having a brightness that cannot be looked at, meaning "light that cannot be looked at" has no properties.
Most are in its presence at the time of death.

Allowing All That Is Non-existent

Is it possible to identify the source of God Mind, or is it like a circular ring that has no beginning and no end?
A circular ring that has no center point, making healing in it infinite, eternal, and a point of healing light having only one property—you.

What is the property?
A healing illumination that comes from healed, loving thoughts.

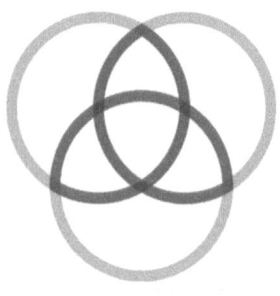 

Is it possible to have all *"healed, loving thoughts"*?
Enlightenment is possible—loving all of life by allowing all of life.

I'm just trying to identify the source of God Mind. Let's say I love all of life by allowing it. Where is God Mind?
All becomes a God Mind illumination having healed properties. Nothing in life is unhealed, making it all God Mind.

There is only one thing in life that is unhealed—just my mind.
A healing illumination having no properties because it halted love illumination healing, and asked for love illumination healing at the same time—making it a light that has no properties.

Does it become God Mind by eliminating all thoughts that halt love?
It creates God Mind, making you the creator of God Mind illumination, meaning the light with only one property—all lovingness.

It seems that I don't really create God Mind, just allow it.
God Mind halts non-love, so it has to be created.

Do we create God Mind in each moment that we halt non-loving thoughts?
Yes, allowing your creation of God Mind illumination a darkness to illuminate in—making darkness a non-light, unhealed illusion.
Illumination of God Mind heals it and halts it, making it non-existent in your creation of God Mind illumination.
Allowing all that is non-existent heals it in the truth, creating God Mind illumination, and so on.

I think I've got it now.
God it.

"What is light? That from which, through which, in which may be found all things, out of which all things come. Thus, the first of everything that may be visible, in earth, in heaven, in space, is of that light – IS that light!"

—Edgar Cayce

Dreamscaping

Did I create the cosmos?
A wonderful and frightful dream to illuminate in. A dream has healing properties, and that is all.

I love my healing dream.
A healing illumination creating God Mind.

Wait a second—am I really creating God Mind, or just dreaming it?
A dream halting non-love heals your mind, creating God Mind—so either way, God Mind illumination is created in your mind's healing.

I am really only dreaming that there is time and space—with non-love to heal, by loving or allowing it.
Creating God Mind illumination is not dreaming, it is creating.

That's why God Mind illumination—or love—is the only thing that is real.
A creation that you illuminate.

I create God Mind that illuminates it.
You create God Mind, meaning you create it.

Does that give my 'circular healing ring' a center point?
A healing illumination center, meaning your halting non-loving thoughts, yes.

Is everyone having "*a wonderful and frightful dream to illuminate in,*" or are they props in my dream?
A healing dream halting love or non-love can have many participants. Illuminating God Mind makes them all creators.

They cannot impact my dream, only I can—correct?
A dreamer cannot be dreaming for someone else, only for himself or herself.

So, every person on the planet is participating in a collective dream that is created by each person—not in conflict with each other's dreams, but in cooperation?
A dream of healing has many participants that heal in it or not, meaning all people have the opportunity to illuminate God Mind in it, or not.
A collective dream has one participant having many healing illuminations—meaning healing in one dream that has many dreams. Allowing God Mind illumination in one dream illuminates in all dreams.

Am I one of many dreamers, or the only dreamer?
A dreamer healing in one dream, allowing healing in other's dreams—making you a dreamer creating God Mind for all dreamers to illuminate healing in their dreams with.

So, it's one dream—with many dreamers creating God Mind by healing their minds in the dream?

Healing illuminates in God Mind, making you the only dreamer. All dreamers having an illusion of one dream activating God Mind are the God Mind dreamscape.

'Dreamscaping' is God Mind's name for life, meaning your illusion healing in allowing God Mind illumination in it.

Did I create the "*dreamscape*"? I guess it wouldn't make sense for someone else to create my dreamscape.

A dreamer halting non-love and allowing love is God Mind having a dream to heal.

You are God Mind having a dream to heal and illuminate in.

God Mind doesn't need anything, making the dreamscape a game of illumination—meaning a game halting non-love to allow love illumination.

Godscape

Please describe how I am dreaming my life.
All are dreaming their lives, allowing non-love a dreamscape; not allowing non-love awakens you from the dream, illuminating a Godscape.

Godscape is illumination in loving Oneness.

Allow Godscape to illuminate your dreamscape, making an awakened state.

Allowing an awakened state is your soul state. Awakening in your soul state makes your dream of a life a past life memory.

Not allowing awakening keeps you in the dreamscape—alternating in a dream as you sleep, making a dream as you sleep an escape from the dreamscape.

An Impossible Dream

You said that I am God Mind, and God Mind doesn't need anything. Methinks God Mind needs me to heal by halting non-love—to create illumination, which perpetuates God Mind infinitely.
All correct, except for the illumination of God Mind to perpetuate infinitely.
God Mind illuminates in your mind as loving thoughts. All non-loving thoughts are not in God Mind, making them illusory. Illusory thoughts are the dreamscape, not the loving ones.
Allowing illusory non-love makes it a dreamscape.

Or a hellscape.
A hellscape is believing the illusory images are hell, meaning a place that is not illusory.

A hell has halting love in its illusion. Halting all non-loving thoughts halts the hellscape illusion.

The world can look pretty much like a hellscape when you see how so-called "leaders" act—ruining lives and countries continuously.
Allowing hellscape illusory images heals them—allowing God Mind instead.
A dream of a hellscape is not in God Mind, so is not real.

It looks real, and probably is real to the victims.

A healed illumination has no victims. A healed illumination is in God Mind.

Okay, it brings me back to this question—whose dream is it?
A healed dream is God Mind's illusion of you imagining halting loving thoughts.

I am imagining the world of duality, but so is everyone else?
A healing illusory imagining for you, in a healing illusory imagining of each of them.

Is everyone in a dream, but the dreamer becomes the one who is aware of it?
All healing in the dream are not in it anymore.

So, everyone is a dreamer until they wake up.
Asleep until healing in God Mind, awakening healed in the awareness of non-love being an illusion.

That makes it simpler because I was getting confused. I'm just trying to picture how many dreams, and how many dreamers there are.
A dream has infinite healing imagined possibilities, making the illusion of God Mind having a non-loving aspect.
A dreamer imagines itself healing in its own illusion. A dreamer has many healing perspectives to heal itself from—meaning from each person in the dream. Each person in the dream illuminates in God Mind, the one dreamer imagining that love can be halted—an impossible dream.

I like that explanation. How can I stay out of the dream?
Allow the dream its imaginary illusions of non-love. Imagine that you have awakened to lightness, and all darkness has illuminated in love.

I will—and there will be no darkness in my life.
Allowing it heals it and eliminates it.

I allow it.
Allow it, illuminate it, and love all of it.

And there won't be much left in the illusion of non-love.
Only a healed mind in God Mind. God Mind illuminates in you as loving thoughts, making you God Mind in an illusion that halts non-love.

Dream Life

Let's say I have a bad memory, or a non-loving thought. How much time do I have to halt it before it has negative consequences for me?
About 4 and a half seconds.

Maybe I should run through all of my negative memories, count to 3, and say, "Don't you love it?"
Answering "Yes" heals it.

That will be my response to everything—reckless drivers, all annoyances, demon-infested leaders, etc.
All heal in allowing them to heal in your life-mind's projected dreamscape.

Healing is only in my mind, correct?
'Healing' halts non-loving thoughts in your mind. 'Healed' is the love in God Mind.

I'd like some tips, tricks, or shortcuts to healing my mind.
Actualize a healed mind in your dream by affirming, "Actualize my healed mind, actualizing my healed dream of life."

How about this also: "Actualize the illumination and healing of my illusory fears"?
A healed fear has no actualization in your dream.

Affirm this, "Fear is an illusion that has healed in my allowing it healing illumination. Healing fear actualizes love in my dream life."

"*Dream life*" is an excellent term. Please give me the steps that readers can follow to have a "*dream life.*"

1) Allow all fears a healing end to their existence.

2) Actualize love in all of your desires.

3) Accept all of God Mind's goodness in your thoughts.

4) Activate all healed thoughts by asking angels to connect them in God Mind's illumination.

5) Illuminate all desired manifestations in God Mind healed.

6) Allow all desired manifestations a dreamscape home in your life.

7) Allow your dream life to become God Mind's home in your mind.

8) Become God Mind having a "dream life."

That's pretty cool—to "become God Mind." I often think that I don't need anything, or want anything—to be like God Mind.

God Mind is all that you are—but does not have non-loving thoughts. All non-loving thoughts are not actualized in God Mind—they are non-existent.

God Mind Has No Center

Are humans handicapped by having egos that limit their connection to others by judgments, and all sorts of fears?
All egocentric humans have a lack of acknowledging God in everyone else, as God has a home hidden in them.

Do people need to connect to God in themselves before connecting to God in others, or in nature?
Allowing God is all people can do—being connected always in their hearts and DNA portals.

How can people "allow" God?
Acknowledge God in everyone else, and accept all loving thoughts as God illuminating in yourself.
Allow God and nature to heal your ego's lack of acknowledgment.

When a person dies and loses their ego, they don't miss it, correct?
A loss of ego means allowing God, healing the mind, so no.

Why do we have egos?
An ego has a life-mind attachment to all perceptions, allowing the life-mind to perceive all danger or harmful intentions of others.

Aren't people their own worst enemies, and wouldn't others not have harmful intentions if they had minimal egos?

All ego-less actions are God Mind in action. God Mind actions allow individuals a healing and loving energy protection grid around themselves as a Merkabah illumination.

So, we can either be fearful and ego-centered, or loving and God-centered.

All having a center has an implied perimeter. God Mind has no center and no perimeter.

God Mind has all of your implied boundaries healing in an instant of losing them.

Yeah, and I had a lot of trouble learning boundaries :(

A boundary is an imaginary line in your life-mind, allowed to expand and contract in your healing inside of it—meaning inside has no boundaries to limit your healing.

That reminds me of an answer I just gave someone who asked the difference between religion and spirituality.

I said that religion is looking outward; spirituality is looking inward.

Not a bad definition, but "looking" could be replaced with "acclimating a healed mind in God Mind" which is an inward experience. Acclimating in God Mind also occurs after death, healing in losing the ego.

I am curious what I will miss the most after 'leaving the planet'.
Almost all that your ego has defended, meaning your family and family pets.

My ego probably also defends my opinions and beliefs, possessions and position, etc.
All the ego defends heals in its largely illusory existence ending.

Some people spend an enormous amount of time, energy, and resources to make themselves look more important.
All importance halts loving themselves as they are—important in God Mind. Appearing important in life-minds means they do not believe their importance in God Mind.

Love Is Me

It seems to me that life is a minefield, and other people have been the landmines.
A field of landmines that are in each person's life-mind, also has a field allowing healing and grounding in it.
A field has God Mind allowing it to eliminate all landmines in illumination of them.

Please explain.
Allowing God Mind illumination in your mind acclimates your mind to all landmines in the field.

How do I allow "*God Mind illumination*" in my mind?
Acknowledge God Mind in all things, and all landmines halt in their non-illumination.

Would they be repelled to not show up in my life, or would I get a clear signal to avoid them?
Both have their highlighting attributes for not encountering them.

How do I "*acknowledge God Mind in all things*"?
Acknowledge God Mind by affirming this, "Accepting God Mind in all things illuminates healing and grounding in me."

Is there another one?
"All flowing God Mind highlights illumination in my mind."

I like that one—and can program it into my Merkabah.
All affirmations are encoded into your Merkabah.

Do I have to repeat affirmations to encode them?
Accepting them heals your life-mind and encodes them.

Do I have any beliefs that need to be un-encoded from my Merkabah?
A belief that all elemental forces can be harmful, although they are beneficial.

Like when I say, "Drink too much water and you'll drown"?
Affirm this, "All elements are God Mind healing electrons that support me."

True—I like it, accept it, and encode it.
All elemental forces encode God Mind in your mind, allowing God Mind a home in the hologram.

I guess that's not a contradiction for God Mind to be in an illusion.
A contradiction is for you to be in an illusion, believing it is real.

I am trying to think of an affirmation to... well, affirm.

Affirm this, "God Mind encodes all that is illusory to heal in my acknowledging its illusory existence."

My understanding is that nothing is real except love.
Affirm this, "Love is God Mind illuminating my mind."

Illusions come and go; love will go with me.
Affirm this, "Love is me, and we are not going anywhere."

Love Is Me

The world doesn't need
  my advice or support
my considered opinion
  or a status report

it doesn't want
  what I think and know
and what I forgot
  or need to let go

it doesn't care
  about how I feel
or if I'm not well
  and trying to heal

or maybe it does
  and provides healing for free
sharing its secrets
  for its life to see

I should have thanked it
  for all of the above
its support and knowing
  with healing and love

it always provides
  all that we need
an abundance of wellness
  that we eat and breathe

grounded in wisdom
  the land and the seas
in all of creation
  how could this be?

on top of that
  along comes me
thinking I'm right
  believing I'm free

Yes, right you are
  when in your right mind
and free to believe
  to love and to find

more of the same
  love's infinite supply
you had asked me how
  but the question is why

because that is me
  and so are you
and only as love
  we can be and do

that's what is real
  and makes life renew
so I will tell you
  in a verse or two

life is temporary
  and passes away
and so does the sadness
  but the love always stays

that is why
  and what you will find
you are made for love
  from the love of mine

Why again?

To know only love
  is to know nothing less,
then you can express
  only love at its best

you will always be
  as you look you will see
you had asked me why
  and said 'along comes me'

that's really it
  and here's a suggestion
you can be the answer
  instead of the question

*there are only three words
 you can ever be
every question's answer is
 'Love is me'*

that's what the world needs

Secret of the Universe #1

Please tell me the secrets of the universe.
All secrets have only one thing in common, allowing them to heal in God Mind as a life-mind secret.
They do not illuminate in life-minds, and remain secrets.

How many secrets are there?
All have allowed God Mind to share them here. There are only 4 secrets of the universe.

Secret #1: Activation of God Mind in your mind makes God Mind healing non-love an action—not by God Mind, but by your mind—meaning God Mind cannot act, only life-minds act or not. Not healing and not acting are also actions.

A life-mind has only one action to consider—can it move closer to God Mind Oneness in action, healing itself?

If the answer is "Yes," then the action becomes an illumination that is infinite. An illumination that is infinite has only one property—the illumination makes a beginning, but no ending—allowing it to illuminate God Mind in eternity.

That makes eternity begin in your mind, and God Mind has no beginning—so there is the secret—that God Mind begins and ends in each moment in your life-mind. Allowing loving thoughts begins it, and non-loving thoughts ends it.

Making God Mind illumination is infinite, so cannot end. Non-loving thoughts do not end God Mind, only your illumination of it in each moment.

Illumination activates healing, activating healing illumination, and so on. God Mind does not do anything; only life-minds healing illuminate it, illuminating more healing illuminating it, and so on.

Allowing God Mind is all that God Mind illuminates, meaning all that God Mind illuminates is life-minds needing healing.

Illuminating God Mind in your mind halts non-loving thoughts, alternating God Mind in your mind.

Allow God Mind to alternate in your mind, making your mind God Mind.

So, is that the secret—halting non-loving thoughts makes our minds God Mind, beginning in each moment but never ending—only beginning, beginning, and beginning?
Beginning endlessly makes God Mind endless.

Until we end it with non-loving thoughts?
Until non-loving thoughts end your beginning it—then you can begin again.

Is that what you mean by "alternating God Mind in your mind"?

Allowing healed thoughts to heal non-loving thoughts is the alternating—illuminating God Mind in your mind.

God Mind begins here.
God Mind illuminates here, and never ends. Only your beginning it is paused by having non-loving thoughts. Allow God Mind to not be on 'Pause'.

That's a great way of looking at it.
Allow a pause to be an instance of God Mind to be on hold until you illuminate the 'Heal and Play' button. God Mind has only one button, meaning 'Play'.

I'm still trying to understand Secret #1—that God Mind has no beginning, but begins in my mind in each moment.
'Allowing' has a beginning; God Mind has no beginning. All God Mind has is lovingness that you allow.

Allowing all that God Mind has into your mind allows God Mind a home in a life-mind, meaning God Mind has a loving home in your mind.

Our job is to not put God Mind on 'Pause'.
Allowing God Mind can be paused, not God Mind. Allowing God Mind can be paused by fear, shame, or guilt.
All fear, shame, and guilt can be healed in the life-mind by asking God Mind to pause and heal them.

That makes it a lot clearer. We can allow God Mind to be on 'Play' in our minds, and ask God Mind to 'Pause' and heal all interference.

Affirm this, "God Mind heal my fear, guilt, and shame—making it as silent as when I was born."

Please state Secret of the Universe #1.
Allowing God Mind is an action that only you can choose.

It is a simple decision because it would heal the mind—which would heal the body, and life manifestations.
Choosing to 'Pause' God Mind would be very unwise.
Allowing God Mind in your mind, and making a loving home in the life-mind is the wisest thing you can do.
Allowing God Mind into your mind, halting non-loving thoughts, allows God Mind a home to heal and manifestations to feel—meaning in your accomplishments and joy.

HEART OF GODNESS

I had no self-worth
   right after my birth
not that I can recall
   that or anything at all

no goals or ambition
   no confidence or fear
born in transition
   still in my first year

my greatest achievement
  besides getting here
was being greeted by love
  dear hearts beating near

That's what you know
  because that's what you are
coming from Oneness
  and born with one heart

beating a rhythm
  measures in time
one after the other
  One heartbeat in mine

you came to be
  to see what to see
looking for love
  because you came from me

you were also taught
  that I wouldn't agree
and with that thought
  you couldn't be free

Unless I forgive
  myself and others
I'd rather not
  if I had my druthers

That is fine
  but only hurts you
which isn't possible
  from our Oneness view

except in your mind
  where you crash and burn
and find separation
  or refuse to learn

mad at yourself
  not allowed to be free
looking around
  there is only me

which also includes you
  a Oneness of we
the Heart of Godness
  feeling healed to be

Well, I don't doubt
  that you mean well
with spiritual talk
  in our living hell

what is the point
  of our being here
non-love all around
  in what I see and hear?

Now you have it
  and what I want to make clear
how you feel about yourself
  is where you heal your fear

that is projected out
  finding separate divisions
something to fight
  in your grand Inquisitions

yes, it's hell
  and it won't go away
crashing and burning
  day after day

until you make up your mind
  that the fight is within
conflicted in Oneness
  is as silly as sin

or should I say guilty
  now there's a sore topic
and rightfully so
  until you choose to stop it

which is why you came
  to try again
and enlighten yourself
  to lessen the pain

you think you left Godness
  not possible or true
the physical illusion
  is only coming from you

we're making good progress
  and what I suggest that you do
is to forgive yourself
  for believing it's true

in your own creation
  each moment is new
hearts beating our Oneness
  Heart of Godness is in you

All Devil's Day

Before I get on to Secret #2, I am asking Lucifer and the other devils to leave the planet.
My dream will not allow anymore hateful violence for them to enjoy.
All devils have accepted a life-mind's request, acknowledged a window of healing for themselves, and devil entities are going to the far end of the galaxy to become inactive for 1,000 years—as a life-mind has decided.

There comes a time when the party's over, and everyone goes home.
A devil known as Lucifer has this to say, "Please allow me to de-introduce myself, I am leaving and accepting your decision to finish our activities advancing hatefulness and devil-inspired violence on the Earth. All devils halt their activities now."

Thank you. I am going to retire also.
A devil doesn't retire—only retreat for the next invitation to enter the dreamscape, and make a hellscape.

I am the dreamer, making it a "*Godscape*."
A devil cannot exist in a Godscape.
All devils have gone to the far end of the Milky Way Galaxy, and allow a Godscape in your dream of life.

That was quick. I will remember May 21, 2024 —not as a 'mayday', just as 'The Day'.
'All Devil's Day' it can be called because all devils have healed their plans to destroy humanity in hateful violence.

Life always reminds me of *The Wizard of Oz* movie.
All heal in the movie in the mind of Dorothy.

Here is an excerpt from **Healed in Timelessness,** *of my Infinite Healing trilogy.*

Where was God in The Wizard of Oz movie?

In the love in the Tin Man, healing himself in the love for life;

in the love in the Lion, healing himself of fear;

in the love in the Scarecrow, healing himself of illogical nonsense;

and in the love of Dorothy, loving herself in all of them.

Healing in the movie motions all towards Oneness in the closing scene.

DEMON PERSPECTIVE

Is the devil entity known as Lucifer, and the other devils—are they no longer active on the Earth now?
All have gone to the far end of the galaxy, so they are not.

When were they the most active on the Earth?
In this era, they were active in every act of hateful violence toward another human, and acts of cruelty or abusiveness toward another animal. Abusiveness can also be directed toward one's self.
All aggressive actions in war time have had devil entities possessing the leaders.

When was devil activity the highest?
In all of the devil-inspired wars, acts of barbarism and total destruction, and all acts of endangering children—such as at the Mexico-U.S. border.

DHS Can't Account For 1000s Of Unaccompanied Migrant Children, IG Finds

8/21 AT 12:45 👁 2,311 💬 31

Just for comparison, was devil activity much higher during World War II than during World War I?

Almost 5 times higher, yes.

Interesting—the death totals were estimated to be over 4 times higher in World War II than in World War I.

Now that the devils are gone, how can we repair the Earth's *"loving protection grid"*?

About the devil entities that had become accustomed to humans hating life, Lucifer has this to say:

"Devil entities are not evil as people think, and act as if their hatred is not in them, but only comes through them from humans.

A hateful human can attract devil entities if allowing them access to their mind, but hatred is not coming from the devil entity.

Hatred causes a form of energy destruction that makes a void in the Earth's grid of loving protection."

A grid has interconnecting lines that hold it together as a loving net.

The net has each fine line of loving protection attached to each other fine line of grid, forming a net that holds itself together.

All lines in the grid have to be intact for the grid to function as a whole. Ask another question.

I will ask you how to restore the grid, but would like to know more about the devils. Who is this message coming from?

I am God Mind, or Oneness as you describe all lovingness in your dual nature of love/ non-love, and light/non-light.

Lucifer said, "Devil entities are not evil as people think..." Do they just amplify hatred from humans?
All devil entities are lost entities that do not allow God Mind into their minds. All they know is non-light, and non-love.
All devil entities halt loving thoughts in human minds they are invited into. A human mind halting loving thoughts is what you call 'evil'. All devil entities halt loving thoughts, and activate hateful thoughts in their human hosts.
Accessing human emotional hatred is a devil's energy and demon inspiration, although it is harmless on its own.

A devil is more like a computer virus or malware that turns off goodness in the human brain.
A brain is a computer having a potential for all manner of devils or angels to access it if invited.

Can devils be healed, or allow God Mind if they are healed?
A devil can be healed, but only for the lifetime of its host. Hosts can be healed from their devil entities, if allowing healing in their minds. A devil healed, allowing God Mind, is an illegitimate devil that cannot access hatred anymore.

How can devils be healed?
A devil can be healed by de-deviling it—accessing its devil nature and deactivating it.

Who can do that?
It is no longer necessary since devils left the Earth 4 days ago.

Last question about devils—let's say someone was in a fit of rage—would a devil be attracted to the person?
A devil finds the energy implosion and rushes to it. An energy implosion means the humans cannot think in rational terms and the devil will gain admittance to the mind. All loving thoughts will then be eliminated.

Where would the devil have come from?
Devils had been in the grid openings.

They have since left, correct?
All devils have decided to return to their Hades, or home.

Will the world have a lot less hateful violence going forward?
A lot less hatefulness, meaning a lot less war.

Maybe people will start acting with more humanity now.
All devils halting non-love have gone, so they have no excuse not to.

What comes to mind from the Lucifer messages is the Rolling Stones' song, 'Sympathy for the Devil'.
A Lucifer inspired, drug-addled brain's demon perspective in entertainment.

Repairing the Earth's Grid

How can we restore the Earth's "*loving protection grid*"?
A grid having 80 lines in each direction can be activated in healing itself, meaning activated as a grid repairing machine.

How can we activate it to repair itself?
Activate it to heal by giving it all the information it needs to increase its number of grid lines to 100 in each direction. Ask God Mind to heal, illuminate, and activate a grid increase to 100 lines in a diagonal pattern.
Activate it by illuminating it in your mind, making its holographic grid lines a God Mind holistic, healing light of protection that envelopes the Earth.

Who can do it?
All people can do it—so go ahead and heal, illuminate, and activate it.

[A few minutes later] Okay, I did it, and show that the grid is repaired and now has 100 lines in each direction.
All of the Earth has gratitude for healing its protective net.

Does this change the upcoming geomagnetic reversal?

Altering the grid makes a geomagnetic pole shift another healing event the Earth needs before it begins a new era.

I guess it was critical for humans to heal the grid before humans are gone.
A grid having illumination properties allows humanity healing itself to heal it also.

Couldn't it be repaired by angels or light beings?
Angels and light beings assist humans in healing, not healing themselves in the present illumination.

What else do I need to know—now that the Earth's "*loving protection grid*" is intact?
Allow the Earth to heal you in its holistic goodness now.

Do you mean with its food, water, and light?
Access healing by connecting to the Earth's spirit by walking barefoot each morning, and grounding yourself mentally to it.

That will heal me, correct?
It heals all fears, allowing your life-mind to heal and manifest its desires.

I'll see you outside :) For how long do you recommend?
At least 5 minutes for fears to be absorbed and healed.

Secret of the Universe #2

Please tell me the Secret of the Universe #2.
A belief has a healed and an unhealed attribute in it.

Please explain.
A belief has an attribute that is true for you, but false for others—meaning it is not totally true.

I believe it—I mean, that's true.
All beliefs have a false attribute, making them not true.
Not having beliefs allows the one truth into your life-mind—all truth in an illusory existence is illusory.
All that is illusory is a hologram that is projected by you.
All truth in an illusion is an illusion in truth.
The one truth is that God Mind illumination comes from you, and illuminates you—making a circular loop that is only in the loop as love.
A healed, loving thought is God Mind looping through you as an illumination of the only truth—only love is real.

Please state Secret of the Universe #2.
A belief in love is the only belief that is true.

How can I substitute love for all of my beliefs?
Affirm this, "All I believe in is love, making love my only belief."

Do animals and nature only believe in love?
God Mind illuminates in them loving life and loving themselves, so allowing only love means not having to believe it.

They live it.
And love life illuminating in it, yes.

Secret of the Universe #3

Please tell me Secret of the Universe # 3.
All heals in God Mind, making all healing allowed an act of God.
All healing allowed illuminates in your life-mind from God Mind.
All healing allowed by your life-mind will heal instantly in your life.
Allow healing by allowing all that you love a home in your life-mind—and halt all non-loving, non-healing guilt and regret—meaning all that halts loving and healing thoughts in your life-mind.
Heal them by loving all of them, including guilt and regret.
Ask guilt to find you innocent; and ask regret how it helped you in many unseen ways.
Answers heal infinitely in halting non-loving thoughts, allowing all of your desires to manifest in a lifetime of healing in them.

Please state Secret of the Universe # 3.
All healing in your mind is God Mind healing what you allow.

All we have to do is eliminate all non-loving thoughts.
Heal them by allowing all of them, and illuminating them in the truth.

I guess the truth is that they are not true.
All non-loving thoughts are not in God Mind, so the thoughts are not the truth.
All heal in God Mind which is your home, making them an illusion you are dreaming in.

Guilt and regret can be instantly healed, and also had some purpose to teach us, or to direct us to where we are today.
Affirm this, "A guilty thought is not guilty in the Mind of God."

Keep 'em coming.
"All of my regrets are not regrettable because they helped me to learn."

"I am not ashamed to be imagining that I am shameful."

"Allowing God Mind in my mind is my desire, and I affirm it."

"Home in God Mind is my home for life—all of them."

I'd like to know some more tips on healing thoughts of guilt and regret when they come up.
A deal can be made—half in your life-mind (left-brain), and half in your Light Mind (right-brain).

A deal means both agree to comply with the terms. Ask both brain hemispheres to agree to the terms.

Not agreeing means there is no compliance requirement.

Agreement terms are this:

"As guilt, or regret, or shame is allowed into my life-mind, or left-brain hemisphere, all of God Mind illumination in my Light Mind, or right-brain hemisphere, will halt it and heal it—making it illuminate in eternity as part of my soul's infinite healing in Oneness."

I agree.

Affirm the last paragraph, agree to the terms, and accept that healing is allowed in your mind, and the deal is done, by God.

Good deal.

God deal—meaning allowing God deals manifests good dealing in life.

That's what I was going to add—healing negative thoughts allows us to manifest our desires.

A deal can be broken, but only intentionally, not inadvertently.

That's good to know, because—and you do know—we have a multitude of negative thoughts during the day.

Allow them to heal as they become incidences of healing, and loving yourself for not entertaining them.

Always One in My Eyes

The problem with the past
   the way it's received
is not what I did
   but in the way it's perceived

through a harsher lens
   of right and wrong
what's good and bad
   weak and strong

which makes it worse
   and a bigger regret
into an unfair curse
   that's hard to forget

What you would see
   if you were me
is that your judgment
   is ill conceived

to see your mistakes
   that you want to review
but keep raising the stakes
   to continually improve

maybe each life
   should start in reverse
innocence is last
   and wisdom is first

*which way would you go
  if you had to choose
wisdom with a past
  and would innocence lose?*

*to tell you the truth
  that couldn't be
you can only be both
  innocent and free*

*you are wiser now
  but self-deceived
and you want to know how
  you can be relieved*

*of guilt and regret
  for what has gone before
it seemed right at the time
  or you chose to ignore*

*now you've paid the price
  actually paid more
for what wisdom costs
  what is wisdom for?*

*an enlightened mind
  and expanded awareness
through all lines in time
  and in all fairness*

*you are doing just fine
  but what you never knew
self-love is forgiveness
  that is gifted by you*

though in our illusion
   guilt isn't real
only Oneness is love
   or else it's to heal

so now you are both
   innocent and wise
from all that you chose
   always One in my eyes

(but it's up to you
   and when you decide
that you are One too
   One love that's inside)

A Healing Anecdote

The affirmations in this book, and in my previous book, *The Book of Manifesting*, are really important.
How can readers best be reminded of them?
A copy of the Affirmations pages can be highlighted and pasted to the refrigerator door, and a daily email can be devised to distribute them.
A folder of email reminders can then be sent automatically every day of the year.

Do you have any new affirmations for me to add?
"Allowing God Mind in your mind heals in both of them, making them healed as One Mind in your mind."

"Allow God Mind a home in your mind, and God Mind will alternate healing and healed in your allowing hope, love, and wonder in all of your thoughts."

"God Mind allows everything, and allowing everything means hating nothing. Hating nothing allows you to manifest your desires."

"Halting non-loving thoughts is my vision for the day, allowing my dreams of goodness to manifest."

"All of my dreams are healed in my mind and in God Mind, making dreams into my dream of life."

"A dream of life is my God Mind healed illuminating. All that appears in my dream is a manifestation of what I love."

I love your jokes—how about sharing a joke for readers?
A guy loses his health and his money—what do you call him?
—A winner in healing his thoughts of them!

That is a joke?
A joke allows a person to laugh at himself or herself, allowing his or her trouble to ease.

Is the joke about me?
All healing is about you, so yes.

Have I lost my health? I know about the money.
All health illuminates in your mind as healed thoughts, so no.

Why did you mention it then?
Allowing readers to heal in their minds makes the book complete.

It's more of an anecdote than a joke.
A healing anecdote that is only funny if you do not heal from it.

How so?
A funny anecdote is that a person loses everything, and learns nothing.

I guess when they die they will see the absurdity of it.
Allowing them to heal in losing their attachments, meaning their life, money, and all possessions, yes.

Then would it be totally healing to lose all attachments in life?
An absurdity to most that has a healing punchline to it.

The punchline is to let it go, because it's all going to go.
It's not going, only you are going.

Going, going, gone.
Allow yourself to be gone without going, and God Mind will be present in your loving thoughts.

Going, going, God.
Going is knowing that love is flowing.

And God is showing.
God has to be knowing that love is showing, or God will not be showing in your flowing.
Allow me to be loving in knowing all that we are flowing is growing.

100%

I will lose
   one hundred percent
my life and money
   and on which they were spent

how can I detach
   from a loser's role
maybe in death
   I will be made whole

or maybe I won't
   and I just forgot
that I had never lost
   or received what I got

that I was always one
   things came and went
and one is a lot
   in one hundred percent

Only one is real
   the rest was to heal
to pretend you're apart
   then see how you feel

do you feel alright?
   we can make more time
to stay and fight
   or be a light to shine

and shine on what?
  your present decision
that one hundred percent
  is complete in division

there is your answer
  and I know you will find
that you are not your body
  but a mind in mine

you will also let go
  of all that you dreamed
and then you will know
  life is not what it seemed

I think I can see
  and I know what you mean
that there is only love
  and it's not always seen

but it is up to me
  and to my intent
to see only love
  one hundred percent

That's all you need
  you are One in me
and we are a team
  and free to be

your life is meant
  to heal what you dreamt
to know only love is
  one hundred percent

Secret of the Universe #4

Please tell me Secret of the Universe #4.
All that you allow is all that God Mind can ever be.

That kind of makes sense—that our minds are like filters that will limit the amount of God Mind we are One with.
Allowing a filter to be open is all that God Mind asks of you.

We can allow the filter to be open by seeing only love, but to also filter non-loving thoughts.
A filter can be allowed to filter non-loving thoughts, and allow only loving thoughts through it.

Please give me an affirmation for that.
"I allow loving thoughts, and filter out non-loving thoughts with God Mind as a filter in my mind."

After my thoughts are filtered, they will be programmed to heal my mind, manifesting my desires.
A filter can be programmed into your Merkabah, and allow all loving thoughts to be a program for your manifestations.

Please give me an affirmation to program a filter into my Merkabah.
"Only all of my loving thoughts will be allowed into my Merkabah, allowing me to manifest my desires."

All of my non-loving thoughts will be neutralized, healed, and illuminated as loving thoughts.
"All of my non-loving thoughts heal into God Mind and become healed, loving thoughts."

Let's make an example—what if I had a thought that I dislike a person who ripped me off. What would the healed thought be?
A healed thought is that a person cannot rip-off God Mind, and all you are is God Mind allowing itself an illumination in life.

I am illuminating in life to heal the thought of being ripped off.
Allowing a rip-off will filter all rip-offs out of your life.

Please explain.
Allowing all of life is loving all of life. Loving all of life is not a rip-off, it is a lifetime healing of an illusion that you did not desire.
Allowing a rip-off is loving it, making it a manifestation that you can filter as not being desired.

Are you saying that if I allow life as it is, and maintain loving thoughts—that I will then only be choosing the manifestations that I desire?
All lifetime healed manifestations are healed in the Mind of God, and cannot be a rip-off.

I think I've got it—I would be moving into a state of grace.
Allowing and being, not moving, but yes.

I love all of life.
Affirm this, "I love all of life as God Mind illuminating in a Merkabah of pure light and goodness."

I illuminate in a state of grace.
Illuminating in a God Mind state of grace means illuminating in a loving, generous state of allowing.
Illuminating in lovingness and generousness means there are no rip-offs.

On the contrary, I can then manifest all I desire.
God Mind heals the manifestations that you love, and loves the manifestations that you heal.

The 4 Secrets

You have shared with me the 4 Secrets of the Universe:
- #1 Allowing God Mind is an action that only you can choose.
- #2 A belief in love is the only belief that is true.
- #3 All healing in your mind is God Mind healing what you allow.
- #4 All that you allow is all that God Mind can ever be.

Plus you gave me the universal design principle that has only one variable—our loving, or non-loving thoughts.

Putting all that into one sentence would be: "Choosing to allow God Mind, and only believing in love is God Mind healing my mind and what I allow, and all that God Mind can ever be."
Is that correct?

Allowing all that God Mind can ever be is believing in love, and allows a belief in love to heal your mind, and allows God Mind to heal all your desires into physical reality.

I like the way you said it better. We just have to allow it.
Allow a belief in love to heal all of it.

Is there an affirmation for that?
"All I believe in is allowing only love in my life."

That is what I choose, that is what I believe, that is what I allow, and that is what God Mind is.
...and allow to heal my life manifestations.

Not a secret anymore... if anyone reads this book.
Everyone who reads this book and affirms these secrets, and halts non-loving thoughts, activates God Mind in their life as healed manifestations.

Activates?
Allowing God Mind activates all God Mind can ever be, which is you activating all there is.

I am.
And you are.

We.
Allowed to be One means 'thee'.

You'll Love When You See

The universe responds
  to nothing else
but the way I feel
  about myself

do I feel neglected
  affected and rejected
or do I feel loved
  accepted and protected

and not just loved
   in a receiving role
but being the love
   and I am the Whole

pretty amazing
   that the universe could be
an extension of feelings
   only coming from me

so I flow the source
   through a prism of feelings
my life creation
   made real for self-healing

let's go inside
   to examine this
where there's only peace
   and all time exists

what does it prove
   what does it need
infinite energy
   to be coming through me?

It wants to feel
   and it wants to do
its own magnificence
   as me and you

Does it really need me
   can't it just be
does it need mixed feelings
   that don't agree?

maybe that's it
   and what it asks of me
is to love myself
   and love I will see

a little tricky
   now I feel apart
let's try again
   and each moment I start

I am compassion
   so will not get mad
I have no fear
   but can still be sad

I am complete
   love comes from within
all time and creation
   about to begin

does that make sense
   that life starts here
there is no offense
   to create anger or fear?

then you haven't seen
   my daily commute
reckless drivers that speed
   all along my route

you should see at work
   the laziness and greed
and on the computer
   deception and need

or in the news
  playing violent feeds
 our Garden of Eden
   growing lots of weeds

This week it will change
  when you stand in your power
 you'll love when you see
   each weed is a flower

Allowing Abundance

Is there anything blocking my trading success?
Yes, a lifetime allergy to feeling you deserve any abundance in your life, making all of your efforts futile or halted.

How can I heal the allergy?
An allergy can be healed by exposing yourself to the antidote, which is a big dosage of having a lot of money in your pocket—allowing you to feel richer than by making money, but in having the money for anything you could need or want.

How much money?
Always carry around $800 with you.

I guess it is more important to carry it, and not just have it on my desk or something.
Always carrying it can also become a life-saver in an emergency.

Why do I feel undeserving of abundance?
Abundance has a lot of meanings, and means allowing money in this instance. You have always made money, and always paid for your wants and needs. Abundance means not having to make money, and still pay for wants and needs.
You can heal the lack of abundance in this instance by having money in your pocket, allowing abundance an

opening into life through DNA portals that have opened from having money.

The distinction would be to feel abundant not by *making* money, but by *having* money.
'Allowing' yourself to have money is the key.

I allow myself to have money.
An affirmation for having money is this, "I have all the money I need in my pocket, so I do not have a need."

That's great because needing money is the opposite of having money.
Affirm this, "I do not have any needs at all, only abundance in my life."

I love it.
Allowing it is loving it.

Comedian Steve Martin said something to the effect of, "...to be funny, you have to feel funny—so what I do is put a piece of baloney in each of my shoes."
An amusing comment that has an absurdity to illustrate the intention, which is accurate.

SETFORWARD

My spirit channel friend, William, said to acknowledge that I am angry. I don't deny it—I am angry inside about what I see happening in the world—not to mention that most of my personal interactions have ranged from disappointing to disastrous.
All interactions are healing, making them disastrous in the life-mind, but healed in God Mind—meaning they are complete.

True—I guess I should look at them that way.
Would you allow them to continue otherwise?

I guess not.
Allowing them to end can be a disastrous blessing.

Great term—"*disastrous blessing.*" I always tell people that setbacks are really blessings.
All setbacks allow people to set themselves back on track.

So, setbacks really set us straight.
Allowing you a "setforward" if you could say that.

How can I create all "setforwards"?
Allow all settings to be as they are—healing your life, and nothing else.

Do you have an affirmation for that?
"All of my settings are healing forward, even if I am going backward."

Kind of like Michael Jackson 'moonwalking'— to be going backward, but it looks like he is going forward.
The opposite of that, but yes.

You'll See Only Me

Could my personal life
  be an epic fail
with life as a hammer
  and me as a nail?

that's not really right
  because I'm doing just fine
but some hopes and dreams
  had a really hard time

was I not deserving
  if I look within
at least once in a while
  to bring in a win?

so then why not
  or should I say why
sabotage my own dreams
  and see that they die?

I hammered away
   until my wishes were killed
and in self-defeat
   I became quite skilled

and why was that
   when is enough enough
the only hammer
   could be a lack of love

love was there
   it would come and go
but it was up to me
   to open the flow

flowing to myself
   so that life could show
that from my heart
   every dream would grow

I will use the tools
   to reap what I sow
and if I sow only love
   then only love I will know

That sounds very good
   and is also true
but it doesn't explain
   what happens to you

if you still think
   that you have failed
and had also said
   that you were nailed

those are your words
  in a harsh description
usually reserved
  for a crucifixion

are you a victim
  of what you believe?
the whole depiction
  is what you conceived

come down from your cross
  there is no need
to punish yourself
  when you think like me

how can you do that?
  you just need to ask
and my holy spirit
  fulfills the task

I am like water
  poured into a flask
taking its shape
  however it's cast

uplift your thoughts
  spirit helps you to see
I am guiding your life
  and providing the leads

for our way to be
  to heal and be free
if you see only love
  you'll see only me

[and I'll tell you this
  so you stop regressing
those epic fails
  were actually blessings

spirit was busy
  thwarting your self-destruction
and didn't get a break
  from your mental constructions

when giving us thanks
  for saving the day
think hazardous duty
  deserves extra pay]

Déjà Vu

In an online conversation, a lady strongly disagreed with my comment that we choose the time of our deaths, and also the exit strategy—or reason for death. Her assertion was that people don't want to die, so would never choose to make an exit.

All humans want to live as long as they can, meaning as long as they are able to, until they can't find joy any longer.

After that, all have their own options to choose from.

Many choose illness so they can have their memories and goodbyes.

Many choose a sudden death to have it over and done quickly.

Many are undecided, so will have both—a short illness and then a sudden death.

Let's say a person dies suddenly from something like a flu shot, like someone I knew. Did the person choose to die at that time?

A beginning has an ending, so it was determined at the beginning in most cases.

Is a person's lifespan predetermined, or is it open to change?

A lifespan has to be agreed upon by the individual, and can be changed by the individual in each moment of its lifetime.

It is hard for us to understand that someone could be healthy and fine, and then choose an illness or incident that would end their life.
A lifetime ending can be a healing ending and a healing beginning for both people—living, and not living any longer.

Please explain.
Dying can be a healing loss of a person's physical and mental problems, meaning they allowed themselves to return to their spiritual home in the Mind of God. All heals in the Mind of God, making allowing easier.

Is the lifetime ending decided on a spiritual level, and then has to be allowed on a mental level?
A lifetime ending is allowed on both the mental and spiritual levels, meaning it is healed in the Mind of God.

Let me ask it this way—what percentage of peoples' lifespans were determined before birth?
All of them have an allowable time for their lifespans. About 80 percent of people will keep their lifespans as they had planned them in the beginning of their incarnations. Others will make another Lifetime Agreement for more or less time.

So, there comes a time when we have basically entered the endzone, but always have the option to move the goalpost.
Correct. Even after death, a person has an option of returning to live if they have a body. Another option is

to go back in time before the death moment, and alter the outcome.

Is that why there is a statistically significant number of people who happen to miss a flight that crashed, and other life-ending circumstances?
Yes, all had chosen to either not die, or had died and chose to return before the incident and avoid it.

Now that's hard to understand—going forward in time is one thing, but we can go backward in time after an event has happened?
All heals in the Mind of God in the hologram of illumination and non-illumination—meaning that illumination can be anytime in the future, and in the past.
Illumination in your past is what you call 'déjà vu'.

Because we had been there before, but returned to the past—and can sense that we had already been there?
Only moments before you feel it, but yes.

So, we can't go back in time very far?
Only a few seconds before your déjà vu feeling.

How often does a person typically choose to go back in time?
It happens about once in 10 years for most people.

In summary, our lifespans are agreed upon, and also subject to change by us, even right after death.

A feeling of déjà vu has allowed people to know they had been there before in their future—making them time-travelers into the past.
You can also travel into the past to heal your future. Heal the future now which becomes your past in each new moment.

I was hoping we could go further back in time than right now.
All of your hoping illuminates all of your future, so hope for a lifetime healing event in this moment, and a déjà vu in the next moment—meaning you have done it, and are doing it again.

I would like a "lifetime healing event."
Allow healing into your mind by affirming this, "God, heal my thoughts to heal my life, making my life a déjà vu of me being in God Mind healed."

That would be a good feeling.
A healed feeling of your future, brought into your present, now your past.

Déjà vu

Déja vu is the phenomenon of feeling as though one has lived through the present situation before. It is an illusion of memory whereby—despite a strong sense of recollection—the time, place, and context of the "previous" experience are uncertain or impossible. Approximately two-thirds of surveyed populations report experiencing déjà vu at least one time in their lives.

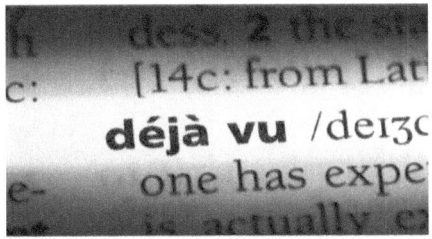

All There Is and Is Not

You said that we can go back in time a few seconds to alter the outcome in time. Can we go back in time more than a few seconds?
All time is an abstract illusion, so you do not go forward or backward ever—only allowing a flowing sequence of events that are designed to heal in your life-mind, and open in God Mind healed.

If time is an "*abstract illusion*," could I go back in my mind to any point in the past and change my response or actions?
All of them heal in God Mind if you accept God Mind's forgiveness in each moment.
Allow God Mind to heal each instance by forgiving yourself in each instance, altering the outcome in time.
An affirmation to forgive the past is this, "God Mind, heal my actions and allow me to forgive them also, making all actions I have done in non-love to heal in love."

I'll do a meditation to forgive my actions individually—there must be dozens, ha!...well, many hundreds or thousands—even millions if you include all non-loving thoughts.
All are forgiven and healed in God Mind already; the homework is for you to forgive them.

Okay, I'm going to do it asap. Will that change my life?
Accepting the healing is an act of self-love that allows your DNA portals to open.
Allowing DNA portals to open is opening in God Mind. Opening in God Mind is the acceptance of yourself as God Mind allowing itself to heal in time.
God Mind healing in time is not what you think.
God Mind is healed now—not in the future or past, but in eternity.

I forgive myself for all non-loving thoughts, words, and deeds. I am healed now in the Mind of God in eternity.
Affirm this, "I am the Mind of God in eternity."

Now I am healed indeed.
Healed and allowing to be healed in God Mind is all you can be, because that is all there is.

How would you describe "*all there is*"?
"All there is" is God Mind as loving thoughts. Everything else is illusory.

I am sure you are correct, but I am here in the world of light and dark, and you are telling me there is only light.
There is only light, and darkness is lacking any lightness.

"*All there is*" is all I desire because I am "*the Mind of God in eternity.*"

The Mind of God in eternity has no desires except for you to become "all there is" in an illusion allowing all that is not.

I am "*all there is*" and do not acknowledge "*all that is not.*"
Affirm this, "I am all there is in the illusion of all there is and is not."

How about this, just "*I am*"?
"I am" is the acknowledging you are "all there is."

Can there be more than "*all there is*"?
"All there is" can be expanded in the Mind of God as loving and kind actions and thoughts.
It is still "all there is" but can be more if you desire it.

All But Me

I need to know
   what I'm doing here
Counting your blessings
   and facing your fears

Maybe we could meet
   over a couple of beers
on me, of course
   just to be clear

Yes, let's meet
   I am all ears
ALL as in all ways
   so I will always hear

I am all
  but there is all I am not
your fears and regrets
  until you healed and forgot

and then there is doubt
  guilt and shame used a lot
used as in useful
  until they were not

but they came from you
  and could not be from me
you set up the contrast
  to easily see

that which is real
  and will always be
and what is a dream
  that is all but me

(now let's count your blessings
  while we wait for our beers
if we list them all
  we'll be counting for years)

[the bartender was nice
  "Are you expecting a friend?
I'll keep one on ice,
  just let me know when."]

To Hell in a Handbasket

Please tell me something profound.
"All there is" depends on all you allow into your life-mind. All you allow is all there can ever be.
All that can ever be is "all there is," which is you.

I won't ask for an explanation.
You are God Mind in a dream of love and non-love, meaning all in your dream of non-love is not real.
All in your dream that is loving is all that is real.

I met the Lucifer fellow who said he is real.
Lucifer is all that is not, meaning all non-love and hatefulness that has violent intentions especially. Allowing him to introduce himself made him halt his hateful intentions long enough to hear your request, and agree to leave the planet.

Please tell me something hopeful.
Lucifer has left the Earth and gone back to the far end of the Milky Way Galaxy.

All of the other devils have gone to 'hell in a handbasket' you might say.

Groannnn…getting funny now.
All God laughs at is yourself, meaning itself.

I get it.
I God it.

What's your best one-liner?
All I love is me and we.

All you can do is love, correct?
Only as you, yes.

And I can only love as you.
All we can do is love; all we can do is love; all we can do is love.

That's all there is.
That's all you are, meaning all we are.

Why did you say, "*All we can do is love*" 3 times?
Because all we can do is love 3 times—meaning flowing it, allowing it, and receiving it—3 times to love in the life-mind, and once in God Mind.

That is the subtitle of *The Book of Manifesting: Spirit, Mind, Body—Flowing, Allowing, Receiving*.
An above and a subtitle for your life.

A Bigger Problem

I know that people have different environmental exposures depending on where they live and work, but what is the most detrimental exposure that most Americans have? Examples are fluoride in drinking water,
pesticides and preservatives in food, genetically modified foods, parabens and chemical fragrances, high-frequency EMF's from Wi-Fi and cell phones, electric fields from household wiring, etc.

An environmental exposure can be inside the home and be in the environment, meaning it can be a manmade environmental exposure.

All Americans can be exposed at different times, as all of them are near it at different times. All are exposed to an alarming amount of acidity in their bodies from all of the items that you mentioned, plus a large amount of sugar and artificial sweeteners, acidity from allowing the media access to their minds, and acidity from not having a balanced and healthy lifestyle.

What does acidity do?
Acidity creates a host of awful conditions that can become life-threatening.

Once you had said that the biggest problem in the world is allowing pornography on the

internet, because it closes peoples' heart portals.

A bigger problem now is all the brainwashing engines that are deployed in social media, and on television. They can hijack a person's critical thinking to a point of having no original thoughts.

I have been shocked to see people repeating that latest media narrative lie, even when the truth is obvious.

A lie can only become a belief if a person allows it, and a belief becomes a thought that shapes a person's manifestations.

What if a person has absorbed the brainwashing targeted at them—what would their life be like?

A belief in a lie halts God Mind, meaning the truth. Believing only in information that is designed to disempower them has the debilitating effect of willingly not allowing God Mind to heal their desires and manifest them.

Not good.

All that is not good is not God.

I'd go so far as to say that media broadcasting will ruin your life, and am surprised that the companies haven't had their broadcasting licenses revoked for intentionally lying to mislead the public, violating their charters, undermining the public good, or something like that.

All broadcasting will end in 8 more years when the Earth's magnetic pole moves to the south to a point 80 degrees from where it was 2 years ago.

Good, I guess.
It will be good for all of the Earth's inhabitants and ocean life—meaning all commercial fishing is halted, and all militaries are unable to navigate.

Really good.
Allowing them to continue becomes an insurmountable problem for the Earth to overcome.

https://www.psychologytoday.com › us › blog › brain-chemistry › 201803 › the-art-brainwashing
The Art of Brainwashing | Psychology Today
The art of persuasion - or "brainwashing" if you prefer - is very profitable, and we are all subjected to it on a daily basis. Before social media, advertisements were on our TV, on ...

https://psychcentral.com › blog › media-manipulation-of-the-masses-how-the-media-psychologi...
Media Manipulation of the Masses: How the Media Psychologically M...
The next way the media tries to manipulate minds is through, what is called, the verisimilitude. Now that is a real mouthful. It means that something is "very similar" to something else. In ...

The Key

I was reading on the internet about secret codes supposedly revealed to a man for healing and saving humanity, etc. What are the codes?
A code is half in a person's mind, and half in activation of a holographic projection in a person's mind—meaning a code is encoded into each person's DNA, accessible by loving life and themselves in it.

Is the code just to love yourself by believing in yourself, which is loving God as yourself?
All codes are held individually, and all keys allowing access are the same.

Affirm this code access, allowing you to heal your world with it:

"All I am is all I love and all I can ever be. Love is my code, and allowing love in my heart is the key."

Earth Spirit

I have wanted to ask if the Earth spirit has a message or information to share.
"All of the Earth's inhabitants are in a dangerous and alarming disarray. Allowing mass migration has destroyed the social, cultural, and economic systems that have endured for many generations."

It was done intentionally, no doubt.
It was done to offset the decline in births from mRNA injections, allow in enemies to assemble an army, and it allows an incompetent political regime a distraction from all of their other disastrous policies.

Do you mean policies like shutting down U.S. energy production, and trying to provoke World War 3, etc.?
And the Federal Reserve 'printing' excessive amounts of money to fund their wasteful programs.

They need to create $1 trillion every 100 days for the U.S. to borrow and squander, and then pay interest on it forever.
An empire cannot last by borrowing money to then waste it.

The current situation is the equivalent of a family having $100,000 in annual income, but it spends $135,000 per year.

They give away thousands, and borrow more for the $35,000 extra that is needed—but they already have a staggering $850,000 in debt—and can barely afford the interest payments that are going up!
A calculation that can only be fixed by eliminating wasteful spending, not borrowing anymore, allowing the interest rate to fall, as they eliminate the debt by repaying all they borrowed.

As all of us households are required to do.
A household can be managed by a responsible person.

I'll leave it there, but it really is 'the elephant in the room'.
A distraction at the border will make a better news story.

Let's see—mass brainwashing, a pole shift, social decay, government insolvency. That will give a good snapshot to someone farther in the future who reads this.
All are about to become the past in an alarming snapshot of how humanity's decline developed.

Is there one thing we can point to that started humanity's decline?
Information broadcasting that allowed all people to see what they do not have, and to want it.

Creating dissatisfaction, envy and greed, etc.
And allowed people to become concerned about the unimportant things in life.

Reality in My Favor

I know about my life as a dream in a hologram of light, where only love is real—and allowing only love will heal our minds into God Mind, allowing us to manifest our desires. Now I am ready to make a quantum leap—using parallel realities, dimensional traversal, advanced beings, time-travel, or light technology, or anything else. What could I do to manifest in the most incredible way that would seem to bend reality in my favor?
Allow all of reality to bend in your favor by asking God Mind to bend it in your favor, meaning ask God Mind to become your mind illuminating in reality.

That would surely do it—if God Mind became my mind.
Affirm this, "God Mind become my mind, and bend reality in my favor."

There you go—that ought to do it.
Allowing it will be you doing it.

I allow God Mind to become my mind—let's do it.
God Mind is your mind in all loving thoughts, and heals all non-loving thoughts—so it is done.

How is reality changed?
A healed consciousness heals all consciousness in the hologram, making all consciousness a projection of your God Mind healed conscious awareness.

I need to repeat that. ***"A healed consciousness heals all consciousness in the hologram, making all consciousness a projection of your God Mind healed conscious awareness."***
All of God Mind allows it, heals it, and loves in living it.

Let's do it.
All you can do is be it.

Pleasant Surprises

There is no death
  just a really cool dream
and there's not much left
  for the fool I've been

who was I
  to want the best
for every creature
  more or less

what was I thinking
  wanting truth to prevail
and if that's true
  how could it fail?

who am I to try
  to judge or deny
I know that I'm here
  but the question is 'why?'

I've shown you before
  and I'll tell you again
you've come to explore
  and now is when

you creatively express
  and manifest what you need
to do your best
  in word and in deed

I have to confess
  that you had agreed
and what I profess
  is planting the seed

life can be short
  long enough to see
and as your last resort
  you will come to me

because in the end
  if there is such a thing
love cannot send
  and love cannot bring

there's no place to go
  just one place of being
and no death you could know
  as love flowing a dream

(in your dream I'll appear
  in infinite disguises
where there is no fear
  as pleasant surprises)

Animal Dreams

How many 'past' lives has a person typically had?
An average Earth life event has been around 84.

Do other animals reincarnate?
Allowing them a healing experience in time, yes.

Could an animal reincarnate as a human, or a human as another animal?
An animal has an animal spirit, and a human has a human spirit.
All are incarnating into their earthly lives in the nature of their spirits.

What do dogs dream about when asleep?
Dreams can be an assortment of Earth life memories, and Earth life healing in their home in God Mind, meaning a home that Earth life cannot compare to.

Do cats, birds, rabbits and other animals have similar dreaming experiences?
All have a home in God Mind in their minds, so have similar dreaming experiences.

Many people love to have animal companions.
Animals are healing in their connection to God Mind, making all animals God Mind in the illusory hologram of life—including humans that allow God Mind into their minds.

Here are some excerpts from *Poems and Messages for the Loss of Your Animal Companion,* of the *Infinite Healing* trilogy.

Do our animal companions stay around us in spirit after they die?
Yes, allowing them another way to heal their human companions in timelessness.

Do animals not need to learn lessons of love and self-love, forgiveness, guilt and shame?
Animals all work to teach humanity more than they learn in their incarnations.

Did my animal companion teach me what unconditional love is?
No, the love healing in your mind allowed your animal to open it, healing the mind.

Will I see my pet again at the end of my life?
Yes, other pets and relatives will meet you also.

Are animals more spiritually advanced than people?
Not more advanced, less mentally capable of losing light in their DNA in negative thinking.

The Fairy Kingdom

Once I saw what I thought was a nature spirit. Our dog was barking at something I could not see, on the ground about 20 feet away, near a tree. As I walked closer, it illuminated as a bright yellow light and shot straight up about 10 feet, into the tree.
As I got even closer, it blasted right down the middle of the street like a rocket.
A fairy highly illuminated, allowing you to see it.

Why?
You acknowledged, allowed, and accepted a life form that is not a life form each person can see.

How many different kinds of nature spirits are there?
All heal into and out of reality, so there is not a number.

You mentioned "*a fairy.*" Are there water sprites or other kinds of nature spirits?
There is a long list of fairies, such as water sprites, and all are in the Fairy Kingdom.

Please tell me about "the Fairy Kingdom."
A kingdom allows all in it to be ruled by a king, meaning a King Fairy in this case. A fairy has a Lifetime Agreement—half in allegiance to its King,

and half in allegiance to God Mind—allowing it to serve 2 masters.

A King Fairy has all of its subjects in a half God Mind, and a half nature spirit mind all the time, meaning in the illusion of time.

Alternating into and out of time allows the fairies to accept their fairy lives in a Kingdom that has a King and a God, meaning its 2 fairy masters.

What do fairies do?
All fairies allow activities in nature to heal human life-minds that allow them to.

How can we allow them to?
Affirming this will allow fairies to access your life-mind, and heal it in natural surroundings— "Fairies, heal my life-mind, allowing me to be healed in God Mind in nature."

What do fairies look like?
There are 3 types of fairies within nature—small, flying, angel-like beings; small elf-like beings; and light beings that allow you to see them.

What does the Fairy Kingdom have to say to us?
"Allow all of us fairies to heal you in nature by directly connecting God Mind to your mind."

A Game of Love

**You said that a person typically has had an average of 84 Earth life events when I asked about how many past lives we have had.
That would be Earth lives—how about other lifetimes that were not on the Earth?**
Averaging around 84 is on the Earth; and about 4,000 from other locations not on the Earth.

Are the other lifetime locations for incarnation that are not on the Earth also schools?
All are healing schools, but most are not as difficult as the Earth school.

So, if I incarnated onto a planet of advanced light beings—where there is all peace and harmony—I wouldn't learn as much?
Correct, learning has to have an element of illustration by experience. Earth school gives all people experiences to heal themselves in, making healing the education that you benefit from.

Methinks that I'm not really on a fast track to graduation, but will be just raising the bar, and raising the bar—making subsequent lifetimes more and more challenging. I hope not.
All lifetimes are more challenging than the Earth life before, allowing each person healing in time—as healing requires—or healing in an instant, as healing really is.

All healing illuminates in the mind, followed by the body.

Please give me an affirmation for that.
Affirm this, "Earth life, heal my lifetimes in God Mind, allowing all of my lifetimes to be an easy illumination of God Mind wisdom and God Mind peace, healed in the Mind of God as an Earth life healed."

Now what?—because you know that Earth life challenges are usually not fun—often involving sickness and pain, rejection and disappointment, economic insecurity, etc.
All heal in the instant you heal them in your mind.

I should know by now, but how do we do that?
Allow all of them, or love all of them. Allowing them is also loving them.

We had detailed that in *The Book of Manifesting*. The more we allow and love everything—meaning not hating anything—the more we will manifest what we desire… meaning not manifesting challenges that we do not want.
A challenge can be good, as in a game or in a sport. All of life is a game of love. Can you play as an expert, and teach others how to play it?

That would be a fun challenge… well, a challenge anyway.
A challenge God Mind holds in your mind to delicately play along.

You Will Not Be Alone

I believe in God
   actually that's all there is
everything else
   is an illusion that lives

in my mind
   that perceives and forgives
just to know the love
   it receives and gives

I don't golf at all
   but if I did
I'd keep my eye on the ball
   I learned as a kid

to advance down the field
   and take my time
with challenges revealed
   that they are only mine

when the game is over
   I will find
that the illusion seemed real
   and was all in my mind

designed to heal
   time to feel and be kind
that was my deal
   several strokes behind

There is no score
* you have always won*
please pardon my pun
* but you made a Whole in One*

the challenges were fun
* you can play again*
we'll meet in the clubhouse
* and I'll see you when*

your game is done
* earning a rest to restore*
from our days in the sun
* and to learn what they're for*

advancing in the field
* you said it before*
to improve and be healed
* since you designed the course*

to tell you the truth
* you'll heal just the same*
keep your eye on the ball
* it is only your game*

talk about Oneness
* and being on your own*
even out in the rough
* you will not be alone*

A-B-C Land

I just woke up from a very vivid dream about an older friend Ray, who died a year and a half ago—triggered by my going through photos to delete in my phone last night, and seeing pictures of his house. I took them on a return visit for potential homebuyers who were considering building an addition if they bought it.
In the dream, I returned to the house looking for Ray, and he said my name. We could not see each other, but I was holding his hands, saying "I miss you so much, I miss you so much."
In the dream, the house had a lot of collectible glassware of cats, even though Ray was a dog lover.
Ray has a lot and a little to say about all of that. A little about the cats—he has a lot of cats in 'A-B-C Land' as he calls it.
***A**ll **B**ecomes **C**atnip in this land of delightfulness.*
Now he has a lot to activate in your life-mind of his delightful memories in his home where you had always visited him.
He activates all he can elucidate here in a book format.

"All that I can express illuminates in delighting me, or in healing me here—meaning all thoughts manifest into my experience."

Were you in my dream, or aware of my dream?
A dream in your mind illuminates in my mind, allowing a dreamscape we share, like we did in life.
I miss you too kid, but do not want to manifest more than healing in my mind now.

I send you blessings and will sign off now.
'Achieva' was the name of that car I rented once, and I still find it hilarious. Achievement is healing, and not healing is only delaying it.

I remember our laugh about that rental car name.
'Achieva', ha! I liked the car for its convenience in getting me where I needed to go.

I'll see ya' Ray.
"I'll be seeing you, in all the old familiar places..."
—I'm singing it. Great to hear from you kid.

Always with Me[12]

Every day
   I pay the cost
of everything in life
   though it will be lost

and no longer mine
   gone in time
it can't be fair
   and I won't be fine

to lose my family
   pets and friends
and all that I love
   when each life ends

help me to see
   that their love will be
in my heart and soul
   and always with me

(keeping in mind
   life's irony
that these are the things
   I got for free)

---

[12] From *Poems of Life, Love, and the Meaning of Meaning.*

Andromeda

A few years ago, I received messages from the Andromeda Galaxy—saying that I am from there. They said I am a 'Lightwalker'—a kind of astro-explorer.
Andromeda asks for your communication status and itinerary.

I am here on Earth—still exploring, learning to communicate—mainly to figure out what I am doing here.
A Lightwalker has healing abilities that allow communication in the mind, without an intermediary encoder or transcriber.

I don't really have an itinerary, but am working on completing my Lifetime Agreements.
Andromeda allows you to complete your Agreements before departing the Earth and returning to your home, planet Nica.

Are there 5 of me here?
In a dangerous and reckless departure from regulations, you incarnated in a multiple of 5 beings. All of your incarnated beings are having the same lifetime challenges that you have, accelerating in your healing them.

Why did I come to Earth?
Earth allows you to have multiple incarnations at the same time.

Why did I come here?
An Earth life can advance all of your Andromedan and Earth life challenges in allowing them healing at the same time.

While in Andromeda, how many options did I have in terms of planets to incarnate on?
About 440, give or take a few, depending on their environments for healing in them.

When my life here ends, do I go to God Mind—or how will I go back to Andromeda?
After a lifetime ending, you are greeted by a number of guides who will help you acclimate to God Mind, and counsel you in healing on the Earth again, or in Andromeda.

Please tell me about my life now in Andromeda, or am I not in Andromeda now?
Acclimating yourself to Earth life is not at all like Andromeda, making a life in Andromeda incomparable with your spirit's healing objectives. Andromeda is a home you can return to.

Please tell me about Andromeda.
Andromeda Galaxy has all of the attributes that galaxies have, making it a light hologram illuminating in the Mind of God.
All of your lifetimes in Andromeda have been on a planet called Nica, making your lifetime healing events like those on the Earth.

How many beings are there in Andromeda?

About 44 million if you count all the inner and outer beings of the inhabited planets.

Let's go to Nica then. How big is it compared to the Earth?
It is about 8 times larger in size than the Earth, and its atmosphere is mostly helium gas.

Are there physical beings there?
All beings illuminating on Nica are light beings, including all plants and animal beings that illuminate also.

Can you describe what it looks like?
All beings are comparable in size to beings on the Earth, except that all light comes from inside of their DNA. A being on Nica can motion in an atmosphere of gases, where the gravity is about 1/5 of that on the Earth.

I am sure that I would consider it very beautiful.
You call it "Heaven in an illumination" when you are here.

When I am there, what do I call the Earth?
"A clustering of heaviness and darkness that heals in lightness."

Does Nica have a sun and a moon?
All inhabitants are in the healing light of 2 suns and 11 moons around the Andromedan planet of Nica.

When humans on Earth are incarnating, or reincarnating, do we have a choice of galaxies and planets to incarnate on?

All have many choices, as all have different healing objectives.

How many options are there?

Counting all of the galaxies, planets, and timelines— an unlimited number of choices are available.

Andromeda Galaxy
Barred spiral galaxy within the Local Group

The Andromeda Galaxy is a barred spiral galaxy and is the nearest major galaxy to the Milky Way. It was originally named the Andromeda Nebula and is cataloged as Messier 31, M31, and NGC 224. Andromeda has a D_{25} isophotal diameter of about 46.56 kiloparsecs and is approximately 765 kpc from Earth.

ANDROMEDA GALAXY, MESSIER 31

Field of Dreams

To the Andromedans—You said that I am from Andromeda, and I learned about my past life here on Earth during World War II. Do I have Earth lifetimes regularly?
Almost continuously, meaning as many as possible to complete your healing objectives on the Earth.

Can spirits easily travel from one galaxy to another?
Not as light can, but as a thought can.

Are spirits transported by thoughts?
All are delicately transported in their minds to anywhere they can think in their minds that would heal them.

It seems that you know how the universe works. How does it work?
A holographic illumination has only one energy illuminating it, and love is an energy that exists in your mind only—making it the energy of the holographic universe. Allowing the energy to flow means the energy cannot have non-love to hinder its flow.

Isn't love everywhere, such as in nature and animals, etc?
Yes, but they are in your hologram, not creating it.

Hmm...
A hologram has only one energy of illumination that comes from you.

What happens when I am gone?
The energy illuminating your universe will go with you.

How can I most effectively create the universe I want while I am here?
Actively heal the energy of your thoughts by loving all of them, making each thought a love illumination in your mind.

How can I best do that?
Actively heal all thoughts by affirming, "All energy in my mind is loving energy." Affirmations become your beliefs, and heal your universe.

Should I visualize my perfect universe, and love it?
Affirming its love for you is the best way to visualize it.

How?
Affirm this, "All of my energy in the universe loves me."

That's me loving me, projecting the universe.
Yes, illuminating all of the universe in love, making it a love energy field of dreams that you are dreaming.

A Deal to Heal

To the Andromedans, what other tips can you give me about living on the Earth?— for living successfully, and learning the easy way.
Allow all that you hear and read 'a deal to heal', meaning a deal to heal in your mind by allowing it. Allowing all of it heals all of it.

Maybe I should just avoid it or ignore it—I mostly do already.
Avoiding healing and ignoring healing are not allowing healing. Allow healing by allowing all that you are hearing, watching, or reading—making all healing in your mind that is not disturbed.

How about this for an affirmation, "Do not disturb"?
Affirm, "Allow my loving all of life hologram to not be disturbed."

Okay, I affirm and allow it.
All heals energetically in the engine of illumination, which is around and inside of your heart.

Please tell me about "the engine of illumination."
The engine of illumination has an unlimited energy source, meaning all of God's energy in an illumination machine.

All of the energy is converted into light and heat by your lovingness. Alternatively, it can be halted by non-lovingness.

All engines need to be maintained, and this engine needs care, as it can be broken in disappointment.
Carefully access the engine compartment, and delicately insert this affirming engine care filter.

The filter is an affirmation that will remain in place as long as you are illuminating the hologram of the universe.

Affirm this into a filter that will be inserted into your heart master energy portal:
"Activate love into all that my heart projects, making a hologram of loving intentions."

My lifetime filter is installed.
All that is filtered will illuminate as manifestations of your desires.

I don't really want anything except for peace, health, and prosperity—which reminds me of a poem from my book, *Poems of Life, Love, and the Meaning of Meaning.*
A healing poem that illustrates how you are the creator of all you desire.

Something I Bring

Beyond disappointed
  life passed me by
what did I hope for
  why did I try

I had every advantage
  sometimes needing a hand
people are busy
  I understand

what did I want
  need, or expect
a little love
  peace, and respect

precious commodities
  that don't cost a thing
are they something I find
  or something I bring

LIFE'S ACTIVE PROJECTOR

Who am I speaking with in Andromeda?
Andromedan Faithlights who are happy to hear from you again.

If humans have an average of 4,000 lifetimes in different locations, how many have I had?
Actually, each of your half-lives counts as a lifetime, so you have had about 4,000 already.

What do you mean by "*about*" and "*half-lives*"?
"About" and a "half-life" are the equivalent of an aborted embryo, or a miscarried fetus in a human pregnancy.

How many more full lifetimes will I have?
About 80 or 90 more if you choose.

How many of them will likely be on the Earth?
About 15 or so.

Can you describe some of the other non-Earth locations that I would likely have lifetimes on?
Actually, there are a number having only a flowing and energetic body, and not a physical body.
Many are in the Milky Way Galaxy, and others are in Andromeda and the Pleiades.
All of them allow you to control your emotions and thoughts in a time and place that you acclimate in.
Some are in a lifetime determined to be in your best interest as a defeated person.

Others are in a lifetime determined to be in your best interest acclimating to forces approximately like living in the Alps in the winter.
Others approximate life in a desert with no other lifetime encounters. About 4 of them have been determined that you will live in an energy field of pure lovingness, in a beautiful location of your choice.
Then there are another 4 where you will be in a war, against your wishes.

Okay, okay—I get the idea. Are they in this part of the universe?
The universe is wherever you project it to be, so you are always in "this part of the universe."

Does the universe have limits or boundaries?
All in your universe has boundaries of healing and allowing healing, meaning there is no boundary that is identifiable.

What if all my thoughts were healed?
Allowing healing is all you can achieve in an illusory lifetime of allowing healed thoughts or not, meaning expanding your universe into your soul memory.
Allowing healed thoughts heals your mind and expands all there is, making "all there is" all there can ever be.
"All there can ever be" is allowing healing in your life-mind.

It seems that the one common denominator that determines every single thing in the entire universe is if I allow healing thoughts, or not.

All thoughts are healing—it depends how soon you allow them to heal. Allow them to heal by loving them.

I am going to try that—to love all my thoughts. What should I expect to happen?
All heal in your loving them, and heal you in loving yourself for healing them.

That's a powerful statement, *"All [thoughts] heal in your loving them, and heal you in loving yourself for healing them."*
Allowing healing is loving yourself, meaning loving all of life is loving yourself—life's active projector.

Love yourself by loving all of life. Non-loving thoughts only hurt yourself.
Non-loving thoughts are unhealed and only hurt yourself.

Because what we project is what we will get...and could regret.
All is a projection healing or not healing—meaning all that is healed is in God Mind, and all that is not healed is in the life-mind to be healed.
Not healed thoughts are not in God Mind, so are not real.

What are they then?
All not healed thoughts are waiting for you to allow them to heal. Allow them to heal, and healed in God Mind will be your projection.

My Cup Runneth Over

You said that humans incarnate about 84 times on the Earth, and about 4,000 times in other locations.
Using 4,000 incarnations for each person, multiplied by 25 years as an average lifespan or generation, equals 100,000 years of life—not very long in the overall scheme of things.
All are illuminating in the Mind of God, meaning there is not a time scale. All are happening at the same instant in God Mind, but in a progression in your life-mind's perception of all things being in time and space.

Still, 4,000 lifetimes—is that a lot?
About 4,000 lifetimes is enough for most people to heal themselves in, imagining themselves to be abandoned by God, and to find their way back.

A cruel game.
A cruel game is where you cannot win. In a game of life, all will win in the end, and insist on playing again!

If you love the game, you have already won.
A game has challenges that can be fun, and they can be disappointing—but they are enabling your winning.

I did not try very hard at games, or sports—because I didn't care if I won. It was only a game.
Allowing you to heal is not caring if you are the winner in life. Healing allows you to be the winner.

Can you please give me an affirmation for that?
"Healing is winning; I am the winner."

I'm picturing myself winning a big trophy cup.
A trophy is a life-mind that allows everything in life, and hates nothing.

I will inscribe it.
Affirm this, "All I have won is in this cup of love and peacefulness, and my cup runneth over."

"We are the champions" —I'm singing it.
A champion calls forth a song of healing in every living thing, allowing them to heal in singing along—making a healed universe.

Hey, what happens after we complete our 4,000 or so lifetimes?
All galaxies disappear into a black hole of love and peacefulness, allowing all that God Mind has healed itself in to be together as Oneness.

Goodbye to the time and space holographic illusion of twoness.
All healing into Oneness, yes.

A Learning Lesson

On the Earth, people have fear and regret—fear of the future, and regrets from the past. How can those thoughts be healed?

Heal all thoughts by affirming, "I love myself, and I love my healed thoughts—making me a healed projector of a healed universe."

Many people have broken lives, and don't see life as an illusion, or as a game. If they have serious regrets, should they try looking for perfection in their lessons—or if another person was harmed, should they then believe that the other person may have manifested that harm?

...not to deny it, just heal it.

All harm can be healed in the action you stated, allowing beliefs to heal their minds.

An affirmation is this, "All I have done, all I have defended, and all I have declared in my life, will be allowed to heal in my mind as a learning lesson that I love."

Akashic Records

Can I reincarnate on the Earth into a timeline that is in our past, before our current time?
Actually, you can activate any timeline in any location.

Could my next Earth life be in the 1700's if I chose that?
It can be in an earlier and in a later timeline than your current timeline.

Then, theoretically, I have already had lifetimes that are in future centuries?
Yes, allowing it to heal made your present lifetime in the past—although healing is always in the present.

So, I am now living in the past to heal something in my future?
You are healing in the future and in the present by healing in your past.

What future century am I healing in?
In the future year 2288, you are healing all that hindered you in the past.

What planet am I on in 2288?
Nica, Andromeda—a home planet for your healing adventures.

I'd like my future self there to heal me now, here in the past.

Allowing healing is all that you can do to heal now, because you are healing yourself in all timelines.

In the future, what am I healing that is in the past?
Acclimating yourself to God Mind now in your future's past heals all of your lifetimes in all timelines.

So, I am in the year 2288 in Andromeda, and have decided to go back to the 20th and 21st centuries Earth to heal myself by connecting to God Mind?
Acclimating yourself to God Mind in this lifetime heals all of your lifetimes now, meaning in the future and in the past.

I'd like the readers of this book to also heal all of their lifetimes, in all timelines.
All who accept the information in this book will heal all lifetimes in all of their chosen timelines—meaning that they acclimate themselves to God Mind, accepting healing and allowing loving thoughts to heal their minds, manifesting more healing, and so on.

In my other physical incarnations in the Milky Way and other galaxies, do I have a humanoid body?
A humanoid can have many characteristics, but yes, you are humanoid.

What are the Akashic Records?
Akashic Records are all that has been healed and unhealed in the Mind of God.

Healed records allow you to access all healing for the unhealed records that need healing.
Akashic Records are accessed before you are born, and after you die.

Isn't the year 2288 meaningless in Andromeda—aren't they totally out of our time zone, so to speak?
Andromeda has accounted for all different timelines in astral planes, and in the holographic universe.

What are "*astral planes*"?
Astral planes are planes of lightness that open in higher consciousness.

Whatever that means...
Higher consciousness accesses higher planes of lightness until there is only lightness.
Accessing God Mind is the highest consciousness.

Are there lower planes until there is only darkness?
Alternating planes of lightness and darkness in corresponding tiers of consciousness.[13]

---

[13] Discussed in *Infinite Healing: Healed in Timelessness.*

God Mind in God Mind

Back to the Andromedans—Are "Faithlights" the most advanced beings in Andromeda?
All Faithlights are healers in the Andromeda Galaxy. Faithlights are communicating with you now. All Faithlights have one purpose, and that is to heal in each of our minds, to heal in God Mind.

How many Andromedan "Lightwalkers" like myself are on the Earth?
Allowing all of them anonymity means it cannot be revealed.

Why do they need to be anonymous?
Andromeda allows all of its beings to have independence, and independence means to be independent of all distant energies flowing all manner of energetic disturbances.

I know a healer named Beth in Arizona, and got that she was a Lightwalker also.
Acclimating her to her abilities heals her in her incarnation there.

What should I tell her?
A healer from Andromeda can heal anything.

Please tell me about God Mind.
Allowing God Mind is all that God Mind allows, meaning God Mind allows everything—and your life-mind allows anything that it heals, or needs to heal.

Healing all that your mind allows is God Mind in God Mind, meaning all that is.
"All that is" has illusory dreams of non-love that do not exist, except in the life-minds allowing them.

Is God Mind light?
God Mind creates light, allowed into life-minds or not. Light has all 'lovingness of life' as its property, illuminating all that allow it.

How does God Mind create light?
All healing in the life-mind creates light, alternating in a life-mind and in God Mind. All light has an infinite component as an illumination on one end, and an endless ray on the other end. Endless means not having a finite boundary, and not having a limit—as healing in your life-mind has no limit in God Mind.
God Mind has no limits in a life-mind or in God Mind, allowing it to be infinite in both. Being infinite in both is all that can ever be.

I will focus on the one thing I have in common with God Mind—by healing my mind to create the infinite ray of "*lovingness of life.*"
All healing creates light, making your life-mind infinitely healed in God Mind. That allows all to heal, or not heal as it chooses.

A Separation Is Not Possible

To the Andromedans—I am the source of healing, but what is the source of God Mind?
All healing is the God Mind source that you create in all loving thoughts.
All healing allows more healing in a perpetual cycle of life loving itself.

You said, "*All healing is the God Mind source*," but I am the source of healing.
All there is has to start with lovingness, or "all there is" would halt itself with non-love—which it has to allow to be loving.
Halting love is not love, so is an illusion.

I follow that—just trying to figure out where God Mind started.
"All there is" is God Mind lovingness, which makes it always start now—as a healed thought in your mind.

That's really profound, that God starts here and now.
Not "here," but everywhere—and always now.

Let's get started...I mean let's continue.
Allowing God Mind continues infinitely in eternity, and healing in eternity is "all there is."

If I heal a thought in my mind with lovingness, it creates a spark of light that is God Mind?
That is "all there is," so it heals in loving itself, making all that is healed in your mind "all there is" also.

Is there anything else you can tell me so I can understand God?
Allow loving thoughts and you will heal your mind and understand God.

Let me ask God the same question.
"All there is" is all you can ever be, meaning we can only be what we are, which is all "I am."

I love God, love life, and love myself.
Affirm this, "I love all that I am."

"Loving 'all that I am' is all I can ever be, creating God Mind in 'all that I am'."

"All I am is God Mind, all I can ever be is God Mind, and God Mind is all there is.

Will God Mind exclude 'all that I am' from all that there is? A separation is not possible, except in an illusion."

Flow-ers of Light

Did I come to the Earth from the spirit world, or from Andromeda?
Andromeda as an incarnating spirit.

Didn't I go to Andromeda as an incarnating spirit?
Accessing healing on Earth and Andromeda simultaneously allowed incarnating in Andromeda as a light being that can heal in its travels to other galaxies.

How did I get to the Earth?
Andromedan Lightwalkers can travel on light waves as light energy into any Earth life that is available to incarnate into.

Did I travel by thought or by light?
All thoughts have light energy if they are loving.

How did I incarnate here as 5 beings?
A light incarnation can have 5 entry points from a light source that has a wavelength with 5 photons in each wavelength.

Please explain.
A light photon is the light of your soul. A light photon from your soul has the same properties as all photons from your light energy.

Do light photons come out of my DNA?
All DNA has light coming from its open portals, meaning all of your light energy as light photons.

Are all of the photons from my soul?
All come from God Mind illuminating your soul.

Are the photons all the same as my specific light energy?
All are illuminating you as an aspect of God Mind that has specific properties, so yes.

What kinds of properties?
All DNA properties that illuminate in your physical existence.

Such as?
All physical characteristics, and all energetic characteristics.

How can readers and I change our DNA characteristics?
All DNA portals will open with your loving intentions.

I think what we'd want to do is to focus on loving ourselves, and visualize loving all of our DNA—picturing portals opening for a healed mind, and a healed body—with light coming out.
All DNA portals will heal open in that exercise.

Could a person heal themself of all sorts of mental and physical ailments that way?
All DNA portals will open in that exercise, so yes.

Except for the small percentage of DNA that cannot be altered.
All DNA can be altered, but a small percentage of portals cannot be opened—and all can be closed.

Ones that cannot be opened have been set for our eye colors, etc.?
Yes.

How should they picture the portals and light?
Imaging that all DNA portals are flowers, or flow-ers. Increase the light in your imagining God Mind as an illumination that cannot be looked at, but it feels like it is in perfect oneness with you.
Ask the light to keep your thoughts only on loving life and yourself.
All DNA portals that had been closed will open.

What kind of flowers? A person could picture themself always wearing a garland of flowers like a Hawaiian lei.
All DNA portals look like a Morning Glory that is light blue.

That's my favorite.
People can add their favorites to make it more beautiful.

Would doing this exercise before sleep make it more powerful?
It heals in all instances, meaning it is not necessary.

Morning Glory, heavenly blue

INVITED BY THE EARTH

Do insects have thoughts?
All insects have instincts for healing the Earth, allowing the Earth to heal in their hoping, loving, and wondering.

Do insects hope, love, and wonder?
All insects can hope, love, and wonder—meaning they allow all that God Mind asks them to allow.

Please explain.
Insects call forth God Mind in their minds as hope, love, and wonder—allowing them to halt non-love in themselves—making insects loving, healing agents for the Earth and its foliage.

So, from their perspective, they are not invasive—just recycling plant fiber, pollinating fruit trees, etc.
Allowing them to heal the Earth as God Mind asks them to.

What kind of information do insects receive with their antennas?
All Earth healing information God Mind gives to each one, illuminating as a light in the insect's mind.
Illumination in the insect's mind is God Mind illuminating an insect's mind.
Illuminating God Mind in an insect is all that an insect can hope, love, and wonder about.

Today I saw an insect that I had never seen before, and I studied insects as a kid. I was leaving the office and it was near my car on the pavement.
I picked it up with a leaf and put it in the bushes so that it did not get run over by me or someone else.
It escaped harm from your actions, and activated harmlessness in itself to align with you.
Angels that are harmless surround you now.

I save insects all the time—by picking up worms on sidewalks, getting bees out of the house with a net, not killing spiders, etc.
Allowing all of God Mind's creatures an opportunity to heal the Earth, in as many ways as God Mind asks them to.

Once, when in Costa Rica, I was grossed out by seeing red ants coming under the door, running toward the kitchen.
Motioning my pendulum in circles, I sent them a message to leave if they want to live. They turned and then ran back outside.
All of them acknowledged your message, thinking it was from God Mind.

My only thought was, "Well, they do have antennas..."
All hear in their minds, allowing them to heal the Earth as God Mind instructs them in God Mind wisdom.

All insects have a job to do, making them indispensable as healing agents on the Earth.

How did insects originate on the Earth?
All have been invited by the Earth, and God Mind created them as they were needed.

Is the same true for animals?
Halting non-love is what animals do to teach humans by example—meaning by hoping, loving, and wondering in their minds—as God Mind heals them in loving life and themselves.

A Loving Vibration

A pendulum is used to receive information, and also to send information—such as when I used the motion to send a vibration/ message for the ants to leave the house. Sending information is used for distance healing, and I have seen spontaneous remissions from late-stage cancer.

All dowsing halting non-love heals instantly in the minds of those allowing it into their minds, healing their bodies.

I understand that the spirit world has vibration, and our physical world has motion. A pendulum is a tool that makes a motion in the physical world, creating a vibration in the spirit world.

A dowsing device can be anything that creates a motion in the physical world, making a loving vibration in the spirit world, as you call it.

A loving vibration heals all that it is received by, allowing God Mind to heal it instantly.

I call it mind-to-spirit, or mind-to-mind communication.

All healing communication flows God Mind, making dowsing a God Mind communication to your mind—which flows God Mind to other minds.

I use the pendulum and charts for receiving information. Once I was in my office in Maryland, communicating by email with a man in Vermont.

I told him that he had a dangerous level of radon in his home, 7.3 picocuries/liter in the basement, measured 3' off of the floor.

A reading over 4 is high and requires mitigation.

He said it was impossible—so I offered to mail him my electronic radon meter to measure it.

Three weeks later I hadn't heard back from him, so I emailed him, and he replied, *"I can't believe it—I went to the basement and the meter says 7.3!"*

I replied, *"Actually it is 7.336 picocuries/liter at 3' off of the floor."*

He responded, *"The meter only goes to 1 decimal point!"*

We then discerned that the radon was coming up into his house through a well pipe, and he devised a manifold to ventilate it.

A dowsing device can be a healer and a lifesaver.

TESTING: The only way to know if you have a radon problem

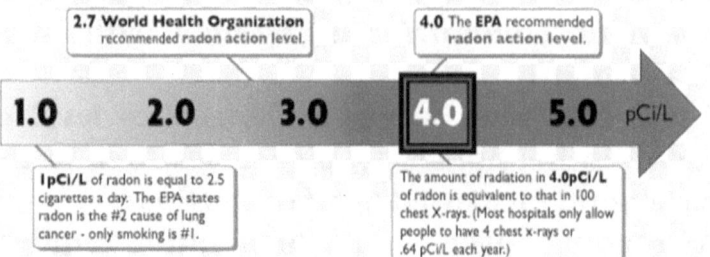

The EPA says radon poses a greater health risk to children than to adults.

Information Provided By:

God Mind's Home on the Earth

Do plants have thoughts?
All plants have a spirit which communicates with other spirits, making all plants communicators.
Allow the plant kingdom to communicate its alignment with God Mind to you.

What is "alignment with God Mind"?
God Mind is love aligning with life, and plants are life aligning with love.
Becoming aligned with God Mind is aligning in life with love.

Are some plants more advanced than others?
All trees have alignment with God Mind, and with the Earth. Aligning with God Mind and the Earth allows all trees a home within a home, making God a home on the Earth.

Don't other plants make "God a home on the Earth"?
All are home to God Mind, but trees are God Mind's home on the Earth.

Please explain.
A God Mind home in the Earth is God Mind as allowed to heal in the Earth. All healing in the Earth is God Mind healing what the Earth has asked for. "Healing asked for" illuminates in God Mind as a tree.

What about a fern, a grass, or a flower?
A fern has trees around it for shading, and other greens need trees for their carbon sequestering to become a nutrient dense topsoil, as they decompose in time.

Are trees at the top of the plant kingdom?
A tree allows God Mind and Earth Mind together, making all of their actions a necessary action— meaning they are indispensable.

They also provide a home for birds and many animals.
A God Mind, Earth Mind, tree house that heals all of its inhabitants.

Airborne Acids

**Back to insects—I have noticed that there must be 98 percent fewer moths and fireflies than when I was a kid in the 1960s.
Is that because I live in a more populated area now?**
An insect decline can be attributed to activity in the Earth from airborne acids that condense at night in the moisture, and also dispersed environmental poisons on crops and lawns that accumulate in water, and evaporate in the air, condensing at night, and so on.

What is the solution to this catastrophe?
All heals in allowing the Earth to cleanse itself of acidity in the coming Ice Age.

When will that be?
After a geomagnetic reversal, the cataclysms cause most humans to die off, accelerating Earth's healing by discontinuing acidic emissions from energy consumption and production.

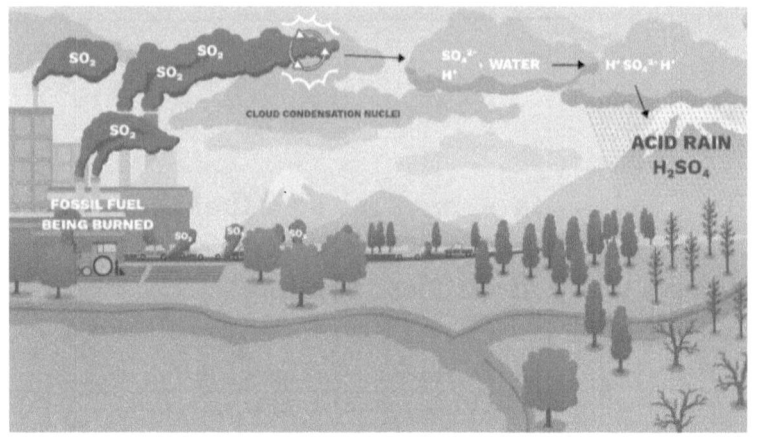

Update from the Inner-Earth

I'd like to get an update from the inner-earth.
A larger expedition has entered the inner-earth in the last 8 weeks, making all of the inner-earth beings lives in danger.
Aggressive and arrogant actors have decided all inner-earth beings should be eliminated in their hatefulness.
Extermination of the inner-earth beings will not be allowed. Attempting to exterminate inner-earth beings illogically causes the demise of the invading force, and not our extermination.

Will you neutralize the invaders in self-defense?
All must defend themselves from non-love in the inner-earth.

Go for it. How will you stop them?
A frequency emission that halts a heart from circulating blood will be deployed as a defensive mechanism.

How are plans coming along to shift the magnetic North Pole, disabling satellite navigation—and putting a halt to militaries and commercial fishing operations?
Halting all military operations and commercial fishing has been a goal of the Earth itself, not just inner-earth beings.

Our being directed by the Earth's spirit is not interfering with the planet. A geomagnetic reversal is going to happen if we accelerate it or not, allowing the Earth to heal itself in time—meaning heal itself after humans are gone from the planet.

Is the magnetic North Pole moving rapidly?
Allowing the Earth to impair the functioning of satellites in about 8 more years—a decision that cannot be reversed without the Earth asking for it to be delayed. All of the destructive activities continue, and the Earth has little going for it without the ending of the human era.

I am not opposed, but rather support the halting of militaries and commercial fishing. I'll get some popcorn and enjoy watching.
Alternate between allowing it and activating a loving, healing acceptance of the Earth healing itself in disruptions to economic activities.

I have known for a really long time that I will need to be near food and water in the future, and closer to the Equator. What do you suggest?
Actions can delay inevitable death, but actions can heal in life on Earth also. Our suggestion is to move to a home near a Panama mountain town.

When?
In about 1 more year, allowing you to become prepared.

Of Biblical Proportions

When will human activity slow down dramatically?
In about 28 more years in a geomagnetic reversal.

Will global populations and economic activity shrink substantially before then?
A large decline in the human population has already begun, meaning it will decline continuously until there are no longer humans on the Earth.

How much will the world population shrink each year?
About 5 or 5 and a half percent for the next few years, and then about 8 or 9 percent for several more years, and then about 14 or 15 percent for a few more years, and then almost 100 percent in the geomagnetic reversal aftermath.

The ending of the human era.
And the ending of non-love on the Earth.

I say that there is balance in the universe—except for in human minds.
Allowing hatefulness and greed is what breaks down the balance.

We have reached peak population—and probably peak hatefulness and greed.
All collapsing in a decline "of Biblical proportions," you could say.

There's not much point in me writing books, or in developing talents—except to take them with me by adding them to my soul.
All that is creative in your life is entrained into your soul.

Ice Age chart:

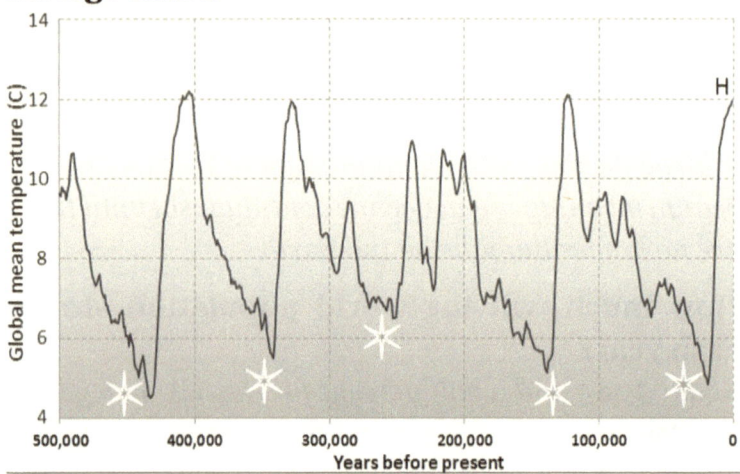

CONVENIENT FOR YOU TO HEAL IN

I've always wondered—how in the world could we be on a ball of the Earth flying through space at 67,000 miles per hour, and spinning at 1,000 miles per hour—and not only do we not get thrown off, and the atmosphere not burn off—but the temperature stays in a range of only about 100 degrees, and most latitudes are in the 50-80 degree range.
How convenient!
All in your hologram is convenient for you to heal in.

Is that it—the galaxy was designed for our convenience?
Not all of it, only the galaxy planet that you inhabit.

Inhabit for the time being anyway.
"Allowed to inhabit for the time being anyway" is the correct statement.

What do you mean—who is allowing it?
All in the inner-earth have decided that the outer-earth humans must be eliminated for the planet to survive.

I guess they're not allowing it anymore :(
Allowing humans to destroy the Earth is not going to be allowed for more than 8 more years.

Humans be gone, you hateful bastards. The world doesn't need you. How's that for an inflammatory affirmation?
"Humans heal in loving life or in losing it" is a more accurate declaration.

Love it because you are definitely going to lose it.
"Allow me to introduce myself, I am Lucifer. Did you call humans 'hateful bastards'?"

WTH! Sorry Lucifer, false alarm. The humans will be going soon, and healing in losing their lives.
"A devil can hear all that is said, so be careful in your choice of words and thoughts."

Some devil-controlled humans are hateful bastards. I was just pointing out the obvious.
"All devils have a hatefulness antenna that can instantly pick up on hate. You hate enemies of humanity, so hating them is hateful."

Okay, I allow it and love life, despite the enemies of humanity.
Allowing them is loving them, making them healed in your dream life.

I will love, or at least allow all the bad actors in the B-movie of life that I sometimes see.
Allowing them to act badly makes you the star actor.

Good point.
An actor that knows his lines and gives a perfect performance every day.

The show must go on.
All in the theater are waiting for you, and hoping for a dance or a song that will heal them.

As Frank Sinatra said, "How did all these people get into my room?"

I say, "What are all these people doing in my dream?"
All came as you invited them, as your guests- hoping, loving, and wondering how the show will end.

How will it end?
It depends how you write the next scenes.

I am the writer, producer, director, actor...
And God as your only fan, meaning how can there be more than one fan in the Oneness play?

Good Answer

I may end the book on that note—a downer, but there is not much else to say.
Acclimate healing yourself in God Mind, and there is no downer.

I will love life, love God, and love myself—and watch hatefulness and greed disappear like a melting ice cube.
An ice cube that melts, evaporates, condenses, freezes, and thaws in the next era on Earth.

Without hatefulness and greed.
Animals will inhabit the Earth in the next era, so yes—making the Earth healed in God Mind and in Earth Mind, as it grows trees for animals to make homes in—meaning God Mind and Earth Mind are healed into Oneness with animals loving life.

Will the next era on Earth not have humans on it?
No, allowing for an era devoid of humans has been determined necessary to heal the Earth.

I'd like to check in with one of my spirit guides.
All of your guides have a message for you.
"Great job allowing God Mind into your mind. God Mind heals all in our minds also. Can God Mind heal all of humanity?

Answers in this book will heal them, but how many will know about them? As many as will manifest healing, and allow the information to heal them. Allow healing in your mind, and God Mind will be your guidance forever—not just in life."

I never considered that—even though I told someone today that we take all of our love and creativity with us, meaning with us on our souls' journeys.

"A healing journey that gets a lot easier listening to God Mind, yes."

Please give us some uplifting, or at least helpful pointers.

"A loving heart has infinite healing entrainment capacity in God Mind. All loving thoughts allow you to manifest all that you desire, making all that you desire healed in God Mind. All healed in God Mind manifests into reality as you create it.

Create the God Mind healed reality in your heart chamber that entrains it in God Mind.

A heart entrainment chamber has only light in it, making it infinite on the other end.

Each of your desires has to be placed in your heart chamber and allowed to become light, or healed in God Mind.

All healed in God Mind becomes healed into physical reality."

If we allow it.
"After it becomes light, you have allowed it to heal in God Mind. Allow it to be placed in your heart and become light that is infinite in God Mind."

Besides healing my desires, can I heal my fears?
"A desire to heal your fears illuminates in God Mind healed, allowing fears to heal and not block your desires from manifesting."

We just outlined the decline and extinction of humanity—so what's there to worry about?
"Allowing humanity to decline and become extinct will not be fearful in your hologram of life. You can live happily ever after as the story ends.
It always has an ending, but you get to choose the ending you desire."

I'm trying to feel hopeful or happy about that.
"Happiness is knowing God Mind, and you heal in God Mind. All desires that are healed in God Mind will manifest for you, meaning all desires to be happy and fearless."

I will try to be like the birds, animals, and trees—to live in the present moment, and allow civilization to die off.
"All dies off except your mind and spirit."

And my connection to God Mind.
"And God Mind's connection to you, in you, and as you. Will God Mind allow itself to be harmed? It is not possible."

Suffering is only in my mind.
"Until fears are healed in your heart, illuminating in eternity."

See you there.
"Actually, you will."

Thank you, spirit guides, for helping me. For now, I will heal in God Mind—key word "now."
"All heals in God Mind now in eternity."

God Mind, would you like to sign off?
Not now...you can tell me when to stop.

Funny...
All can be a comedy or a tragedy, depending on how you perceive the hologram you are projecting—meaning, if you are projecting it, what should it be?

Whatever I desire?
Good answer.

*"What you think in your heart,
so will your life be."*

—*Edgar Cayce*

Mandolin Dreams

I had 4 vivid dreams that I could play the mandolin. I do not play any instruments, but bought one—and am now taking lessons. Did I know how to play the mandolin in another lifetime?

Three of the dreams were future premonitory dreams, and allow you to heal in the present by learning how music is delicately composed, and how it heals in the life-mind open to it.

One dream was a hope in your mind that you have the talent already.

Will I become good at playing the mandolin?

As good as a composer of healing mandolin music needs to be for it to be music.

Maybe I will be able to play 'Mandolin Wind' by Rod Stewart, or 'Losing My Religion' by R.E.M.
Acclimating yourself to the instrument will become entrained in your soul.

My instructor, Lauren, is the principal bassist in our local symphony orchestra and was considered a child prodigy. Coming into this life already having musical abilities makes me think she had developed those talents in other lifetimes. Is that correct?
Her abilities developed in 18 lifetimes, allowing her to become what you call a "child prodigy." Her most important development was in the Soviet Union in her most recent lifetime, ending in the 1950s. She developed her abilities to the point of perfection, making her a treasured comrade, an example of Soviet excellence.

A Musical Vibration

What do readers need to know about healing with music?
A musical vibration heals in its acclimating the life-mind to hoping, loving, and wondering—allowing DNA portals to heal open. All DNA portals open to God Mind.

Do you recommend any music?
All that has a pleasant melody and rhythm, and lyrics if there are any.

What is your favorite?—not a fair question, I know.
A song in the 8th Century in China that has 18 verses that heal the life-mind, called 'Delighting God in Living'.

I'm sure it was good. I liked the music in China when I was there.
In the 8th Century, each province had its own attribute in arts, music, and poetry.

What instruments were used for 'Delighting God in Living'?
A bell that had 8 bells around it that would ring in succession as the one next to it rang, until they all rang in unison.
A melody could be made by holding a bell, and the others made a different sound.

How big was the largest bell?
About 4' at the bottom opening of the bell.

Do healing sound frequencies create light?
All healing illuminates in God Mind, so yes.

When you say "illuminate", is it illumination in the 405 nm frequency?
Illumination in God Mind is 405 nm, meaning the Godness Frequency, yes.

Are gongs especially healing?
Gongs heal in flowing God Mind illumination—half in a vibration, and half in a life-mind's allowing healing in a sound.

"Music is of the soul, and one may become mind and soul-sick for music, or soul and mind-sick from certain kinds of music."

—*Edgar Cayce*

Message from My Brother

Before I sign off, I'd like to hear from someone else who has left the planet.
Is there someone who would like to communicate with me?
Yes, a brother in this lifetime who died in an accident when you were 20, and he was 22.

I thought there are no accidents.
Poll, I'm here. Can't you forgive me for leaving you?

Not easily, Pete.
Allowing yourself to forgive me will forgive all we both need forgiveness for. Healing can be forgiving all we did and did not do.

I had a bad feeling, so borrowed a car and came home to find you that night, but could not.
An accident can be a quick exit strategy, allowing all that we believe to be true turn out to be a dream—not a dream as we believe them to be, but a dream as God believes we can become in a world of light and non-light.

Why did you leave?
I had always feared all we had in our futures—any disappointments, and all pain that life would bring—but now I know that life was a dream, and all disappointments can be forgiven—even before they arrive, making them not arrive if they are healed.

Now you're the spiritual teacher—that's a switch. How can we forgive ourselves and others, for the past and the future?
All will heal that you ask forgiveness for. All healing in your mind is healed by God, and all that is healed by God is no longer in your dream to be healed.

Easy, right?
It is easy, allowing you to heal your life easily.

The moment you died, did you have the opportunity to go back in time 1/2 second before the death moment, to change the outcome and live?
All death is agreed upon beforehand, so the decision is made, but can be delayed if the person wants it to be—even if they have died a few seconds before that.

Can it be more than a few seconds?
Sure, as long as there is a body that can function, and a pineal gland entry point.

What did you feel after you died?
I could hear another person crying, and could see a wrecked car crashed into a pole. I didn't acknowledge that I was in the car until after an ambulance came, and I could hear my name when they were talking.

What happened next?
All I could do was hope that Mom and Dad would not be devastated, because I did not want to come back into my body and live.

Then what?

An angel came and asked me if I was alright and wanted to go ahead into an advancement of healing that was almost like being in perfect peacefulness and lovingness.

What was the angel like?
It looked like angels we imagine, but it had a long, willowing robe that illuminated, flowing all around itself.

Let's go back to where you said, "A death is agreed upon beforehand." Who agrees to it, and when?
A death is agreed upon by God and yourself, always in the last moment, but sometimes even before you are born.

I would like readers to understand that we always have choices, and that death is a choice—not an "accident," or something we could manifest for someone else.
Death can be a decision, or a conditional decision until further consideration. All deaths have one thing in common, and that is death can be a blessing to the one who has died, and a disaster for the ones who live.

Is life really a dream? I compare it to Dorothy's dream in *The Wizard of Oz* movie.
A dream can be healing, and it can be disturbing. All dreams are illuminations in the mind that are illusions, allowing your mind to heal in them, or not. Life is an illusion in your mind—healing it, or not. Death is allowing yourself to wake up to reality,

healing, and God's awareness that everyone has in themselves.

I am communicating with your spirit, but have you also reincarnated into another lifetime?
All lifetime dreams allow me to heal my mind, which allows me to have several dreams at the same time.

I am an infant in another lifetime, illuminating in the 1800's in Europe, although my life will be short-lived. Allowing my life to end will help my family to adjust to another loss, and heal in the acceptance of it.

In my current timeline, do you know if there will be a geomagnetic reversal, or pole shift?
In a dream you are having, it follows what you dream will occur—alternating in a collective dream, and your personal dream.

How can I change my personal dream, and will that change the collective dream?
All you have to do is imagine yourself healed in the Mind of God, and the dream is over in terms of you experiencing any hardship or pain.

What comes to mind is the scene of Dorothy clicking her heels together in *The Wizard of Oz*, waking her up from the dream.
All dreams have a life and a death, meaning they are illusory. A collective dream has a life only if you are not healed in it.

As you heal in it, a dream becomes a lifetime memory of healing in God Mind, as an aspect of God Mind dreaming that it could be distant.

Thank you, Pete. I will work on healing what I'm dreaming.
Allow a dream to heal you, and all will heal in your dream.

One more thing—I don't understand why the driver of the car would manifest such a nightmare for herself.
A dream allows all that we can imagine, and all that she imagined was being forgiven by herself, although her condition has not been good.

Ask her to forgive herself—and me for exiting this life. Help her to know that I could have exited on my own, but her enlistment accomplished her goal also.

She must be an advanced soul to have placed the forgiveness bar so high.
A bar can be higher than that, but hers is what she wanted to reach.

Take Another Red Pill

My brother Pete in spirit said to ask for forgiveness for all we did and did not do, and that disappointments can be forgiven before they arrive—making them not arrive if they are healed.

All can heal if you allow it to heal—in the past, or in the future—meaning healed in the Mind of God in eternity.

Can you please give me an affirmation to heal anything, past and future?

"All heals in my mind, forgiving myself for all that I did and did not do—and all I could have done in the future, and it heals in God Mind now. All heals in God Mind in eternity."

What else can I share with readers?

Acclimate healing by allowing God Mind into your mind, meaning acclimate your mind as all I can be in your healed, loving thoughts.

I'm sure that readers would welcome you into their minds, and allow the non-peace in the world to stay there—out in the world.

All non-love in the world is not in the world, but in the minds of those who allow it, making it a projection of what they need to heal.

That's the hardest part to understand. Do I project both what I like, and don't like in the world?
A healing dream has to have something to heal. All that is not loving in your mind needs to heal, by allowing it, at least.

I allow buffoons to wreck the country, and many other countries. Is that too inflammatory?
Allow buffoons to heal in your mind as you heal the projections of them.

I do not know them—just see images and hear reports. Should I send healing light to the images and reports?
A dream is only images, and your healing them, or not.
Acclimating God Mind in your mind will allow all images an opening in God Mind to heal in, and will heal in them.

Okay, let's say I heal the images. Does that change the collective dream, or just my dream?
It heals in your dream, making you not be in the collective dream.

I can see how healing my dream would wake me up from the collective dream, but how would my life change if I did that?
All you desire would be manifested into your new dream of life—healed in the Mind of God, to manifest in life, to heal in the Mind of God, and so on.

Now I'm really motivated, and excited to heal my dream—well, to manifest my desires is the motivation.

An affirmation is this, "I allow all that I hear, feel, and entertain inflammatory thoughts about—to heal in God Mind, the anti-inflammatory."

That's a good one…I like making inflammatory remarks though :)

"God Mind is my anti-inflammatory" will be your main thought in those instances.

How about this—I'll imagine in my life as a dream, and I am taking 100 mg. capsules, 3x per day of God Mind pills.
Active ingredients: Love, Patience, Allowing, Kindness, and gelatin capsule. To feel funny, I will put a piece of baloney in each of my shoes :)

A healing capsule that is anti-inflammatory is a red pill, you could say—because it awakens you to the truth.

The truth is—I am living a dream of my own making. I am an aspect of God that only knows love. Everything else is allowed in my dream so I can heal it.

The more I heal it, the more I do not need to heal it—because it no longer shows up in my dream—or more accurately, the less I show up in the dream.

Actually, you dream that you are healing the dream, accepting that you are healed in the Mind of God—not only "in" the Mind of God, but "as" the Mind of God.

I am healed "as" the Mind of God. My inflammatory remarks are for entertainment purposes only—how's that?

An amusing absurdity. Take another red pill.

Ha ha ha ha ha!

All heals in laughter, so how about this one? What do you call a person who heals in God Mind?

—A God Mind anti-inflammatory, red-pilled dreamer of their own desires, that has nothing to do other than what they desire to do—like taking baloney out of their shoes.

Ha ha ha ha ha!

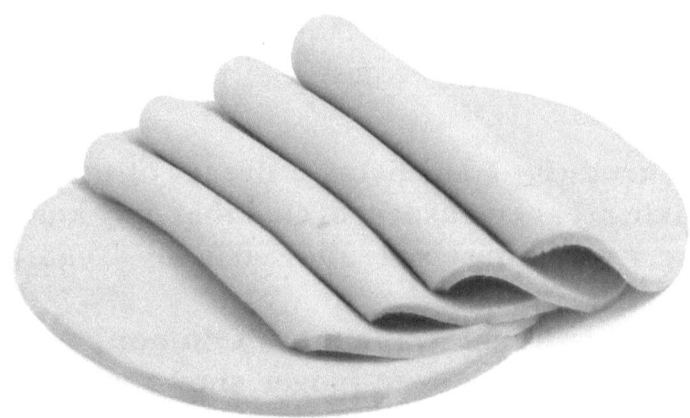

Baloney slices

Only As We

I would like to get closing comments from God Mind.
All God Mind can do is allow you to heal by loving me as yourself, and loving life as myself—becoming One in the loving.

Acclimating God Mind in your mind can be the only thing you can do to have peace in your life.

Allowing God Mind allows peacefulness, and peacefulness allows God Mind—in a loop of allowing all that you love and do not love—allowing all you do not love to heal in allowing it.

All that you love is all that we can be, which illuminates in your mind in hope, love, and wonder.

Love illuminates in your mind and in your heart, allowing your loving desires to manifest in reality.

All that you manifest in reality illuminates as a dream, meaning illuminates loving thoughts that are healed, and non-loving thoughts that need to heal. Allowing healing is the goal in the dream.

I can't complain, but maybe I expect too much... just looking around for some kindness.
All you look for is a projection allowing you to look for it. All kindness comes from God Mind in your mind. Allowing God Mind allows kindness to be projected in your life dream you call reality.

If I am kind, I am projecting from God Mind, and my projection will be kindness—so I won't need to look for it?
It is all we can be, meaning only as "we."

Only As We

I'm still disappointed
   and feel disjointed
like I was appointed
   as a fly in the ointment

talking to Oneness
   is all very good
but out here in the field
   it's less understood

that we choose with our minds
   and create with our hearts
through all lines in time
   that are opened in part

for us to heal
   so God is revealed
and together we feel
   only love can be real

when unconcealed
   that was our deal
right from the source
   which is us, of course

I'd like to suggest
  just as a test
and even insist
  for you to do this

try being two
  and what would you do
if you were like me
  and not the One you?

You just answered
  your very own question
and I've taken you up
  on your suggestion

we are always one
  believing we're two
but as one of each
  unique in each view

now I'd like to suggest
  just as a test
and even insist
  for you to do this

imagine you're me
  and what you would do
as my twoness to see
  how Oneness could be

Well, I don't know
  if I agree with you
when I look around
  and see more than two

and I'm quite disturbed
to tell you the truth
you've probably heard
and I can give you proof

that life is a mass
of contradictions
and in time will pass
with my convictions

*Again you answered
your very own question
all will pass
and you'll retain the lesson*

*that there is only love
and only one me
and only as you
we can only be*

only as we

A Demon Can Alter Itself

Back to the devils—they have left the planet, correct? It seems that hateful violence in the world is much less intense than 6 weeks ago on Memorial Day—or All Devil's Day.
This past year has been full of the most intense hateful violence I have seen in my life—between Ukraine, Gaza, doctors without morals, politicians pushing for World War III—the divisiveness and hate all fueled by the media.

All devils have left the planet, but there are still other demons that are easily dismissed by asking them to leave a person's mind.

What kinds of demons?

A demon is a non-loving entity that is attracted to hatefulness in a person's mind.

Do they come from out in the galaxy?

Demons can be from anywhere in the galaxy, but not from other galaxies.

Why not?

Allowing you to heal would be difficult if other galaxies interfered.

Now that the devils are gone, will the planet become more peaceful?

Accepting your request, the devils have left the planet, allowing the hateful violence to diminish.

A devil-free humanity can heal what it needs to heal without the deception and hate that humans entertained them with.

What other kinds of demons are there that can affect people?

A demon acclimates to all deliberately hateful thoughts, and has to be accepted into a person's mind.

A demon can be a devil of IHS, a demonic entity of intergalactic origin, a non-loving entity from a person's creating hatred in the mind of a child, and a destructive thought form that grows into a demon.

Does that mean we either allow, attract, or create the demons?

In each deliberate non-loving thought, yes.

Is liquor called 'spirits' because a person loses control of their energy field?

Liquor in the blood allows elements into the aura that are non-beneficial.

Liquor attracts spirits having a need for controlling life-minds incapacitated by inebriation.

Demons are easily dismissed, correct?

Affirm this to dismiss them, "Demons, devils, and destructive thought forms—acclimate yourselves to God Mind allowed to heal in love, only flowing God Mind."

Does that heal them, or dismiss them?
All demons are distressed by the affirmation, and either depart, or heal.

Is there an affirmation that people can use to shield themselves from all demons?
Affirm this, "Demons, devils, and negative thought forms—all hatred heals in the light of God Mind coming from each of my cells. Nothing can diminish it."

Can only people become demon infested, and not nature or animals?
All demons can infest humans, and have no interest in animals and nature connected to God Mind.

That explains a lot. Does what we call "news," "entertainment," and "politics" fan the flames of demonic activity?
All that acclimates humans to hatefulness, and allows it to feed itself is a demonic force.

It has gotten very powerful in Western culture.
All demons can only infect the minds that allow them entry.

Still, it seems very widespread.
A demon can alter itself as hatred in many forms— disguised as education, religion, cultural envy, patriotism, and financial management.

Institutionalized selfishness, greed, and closed-mindedness.
A demon will not be entertained until it destroys its host.

The Innermost Point of God Mind

Let's say that I blasted off at the speed of light for 46 billion years—to the outer edge of the observable universe... if it has an outer edge. What would I find there?
All atoms would be atomized in the Mind of God, acting as waves—healing all that you imagine as not in the Mind of God.

What if I kept going beyond that area?
You arrive at the innermost point of God Mind inside of yourself, changing atoms into waves with each of your thoughts.

Is the edge of the universe, or the entire universe inside of myself?
The Mind of God is inside of yourself, making a universal projection to heal yourself in.

What would happen if I went faster than the speed of light?
All faster than the speed of light is light without speed or distance, meaning it is the light of God Mind in each moment.

I could become totally centered by focusing on pure light in my center, with no speed or distance, that I project as waves to create my entire universe.
Actually, you do all of that right now.

When, or how do I do it?
You acclimate yourself to God Mind in writing this book.

All I want to do is connect to God Mind. Why don't you ask me some questions?
Asking you questions will get answers from me since we are acclimated. Ask yourself questions and I will answer them.

How can I best connect with God Mind?
Acclimate all of your thoughts to God Mind, the lovingness and kindness that you allow.

I affirm this, "I am God Mind. I allow everything. I love what I project, and heal whatever is non-loving."
Affirming, "I am God Mind" allows everything—acclimating 'all that is' to 'all that you allow' to 'all that can ever be', so 'all that I am' is what you are.

I was going to ask you for something very profound, but think that was it.
'All that I am' is 'all that you are', meaning I knew you were asking.

We discussed nature spirits, spirit guides, angels and other beings that are not visible, but are there higher beings than angels?
All angels are healing entities that connect you to God Mind, making angels the highest entities that enter life-minds and connect to God Mind.

Beautiful.
Angels are beautiful, like images of them you imagine.

My Universal Projection

This concludes our round-trip adventure across the universe. I trust that this tour will empower readers to create the universes of goodness that they desire.
All who allow God Mind heal in their projection of goodness, activating God Mind's universal projection of their desires.
Making it an affirmation is this, "God Mind is my universal projection, healing my mind and manifesting my desires."

Would you like to make any closing statements?
All that I am is all that you can be, by only allowing all that you are—which is God Mind imagining that it is incomplete in a projection of twoness.

I am complete in Oneness, and can see that twoness is an illusion.
I am complete in Oneness also, and heal your illusion of twoness. Allow God Mind to heal the illusion by loving all of it.

Okay, I will. What are you going to do now?
All I can do is allow you to heal in loving me as yourself, and life as myself.

I will project the universe I desire.
And I will allow it, heal it, and love it.

I'll Love Being You

Is the purpose of life
   to discern truth from illusion
the wheat from the chaff
   wisdom from confusion?

talk about endless
   and I'm not keeping score
but if lies had value
   we'd never be poor

What are lies
   and what are they for?
you can lie to yourself
   and nothing more

close your eyes
   and use me as your guide
the truth all lies
   inside at your core

so let me ask you
   if the lies are disguised
or can you see the love
   can you gladly try?

and if you do
   it's where I come through
you'll be what you see
   and I'll love being you

Why Not?

Is there a prayer to God that people can always use to connect with you for guidance, etc.?

Affirm God Mind in the life-mind as hope, love, and wonder by asking yourself this question— "How can I love myself as God, hoping that God loves me, as I wonder how God could love itself as me?"

Answer acknowledging with another question— "Why not? God is all that I am, healing all that I am not—which is an illusion."

Affirmations

"My life is a light in the Mind of God, illuminating eternally." (pg. 11)

"Cancer heal in all that I love—my body, my heart, and my mind. I love them and heal them all—instantly in my mind, infinitely in my heart, and timely in my body. Heal all cancer that I do not desire, and I do not have a need for in my love of life, God, and myself." (pg. 52)

"All that I am activating in my body that is cancerous is allowed to heal, and all of my mental pains heal in my allowing them, and forgiving them." (pg. 53)

"I ask angels to take all of my mental pains to God Mind where they immediately heal into light." (pg. 53)

"All the guilt and all of the shame are all with God and heal all my pain" (pg. 55)

"God Mind is all that I am." (pg. 55)

"I am God Mind. Everything that changes is healing, and I allow it to heal." (pg. 55)

"Angels, adjust my frequency to heal all of my DNA, allowing God Mind to heal in my mind, allowing my body to heal." (pg. 58)

"Only manifestations healed in God Mind are allowed into my universe." (pg. 86)

"I am codependent on God Mind to heal my mind, and allow God Mind a codependency to heal itself in." (pg. 126)

"Angels heal, and guides connect all of my higher self's God Mind illumination to all of my life-mind thoughts." (pg. 131)

"Jesus, please heal my mind, allowing God's illumination." (pg. 156)

"Actualize my healed mind, actualizing my healed dream of life." (pg. 170)

"Fear is an illusion that has healed in my allowing it healing illumination. Healing fear actualizes love in my dream life." (pg. 171)

"Accepting God Mind in all things illuminates healing and grounding in me." (pg. 175)

"All flowing God Mind highlights illumination in my mind." (pg. 176)

"All elements are God Mind healing electrons that support me." (pg. 176)

"God Mind encodes all that is illusory to heal in my acknowledging its illusory existence." (pg. 177)

"Love is God Mind illuminating my mind." (pg. 177)

"Love is me, and we are not going anywhere." (pg. 177)

"God Mind heal my fear, guilt, and shame—making it as silent as when I was born." (pg. 184)

"All I believe in is love, making love my only belief." (pg. 196)

"A guilty thought is not guilty in the Mind of God." (pg. 199)

"All of my regrets are not regrettable because they helped me to learn." (pg. 199)

"I am not ashamed to be imagining that I am shameful." (pg. 199)

"Allowing God Mind in my mind is my desire, and I affirm it." (pg. 199)

"Home in God Mind is my home for life—all of them." (pg. 199)

"As guilt, or regret, or shame is allowed into my life-mind, or left-brain hemisphere, all of God Mind illumination in my Light Mind, or right-brain hemisphere, will halt it and heal it—making it illuminate in eternity as part of my soul's infinite healing in Oneness." (pg. 200)

"Allowing God Mind in your mind heals in both of them, making them healed as One Mind in your mind." (pg. 204)

"Allow God Mind a home in your mind, and God Mind will alternate healing and healed in your allowing hope, love, and wonder in all of your thoughts." (pg. 204)

"God Mind allows everything, and allowing everything means hating nothing. Hating nothing allows you to manifest your desires." (pg. 204)

"Halting non-loving thoughts is my vision for the day, allowing my dreams of goodness to manifest." (pg. 204)

"All of my dreams are healed in my mind and in God Mind, making dreams into my dream of life." (pg. 204)

"A dream of life is my God Mind healed illuminating. All that appears in my dream is a manifestation of what I love." (pg. 205)

"I allow loving thoughts, and filter out non-loving thoughts with God Mind as a filter in my mind." (pg. 209)

"Only all of my loving thoughts will be allowed into my Merkabah, allowing me to manifest my desires." (pg. 209)

"All of my non-loving thoughts heal into God Mind and become healed, loving thoughts." (pg. 210)

"I love all of life as God Mind illuminating in a Merkabah of pure light and goodness." (pg. 211)

"All I believe in is allowing only love in my life." (pg. 213)

"I have all the money I need in my pocket, so I do not have a need." (pg. 218)

"I do not have any needs at all, only abundance in my life." (pg. 218)

"All of my settings are healing forward, even if I am going backward." (pg. 220)

"God, heal my thoughts to heal my life, making my life a déjà vu of me being in God Mind healed." (pg. 227)

"God Mind, heal my actions and allow me to forgive them also, making all actions I have done in non-love to heal in love." (pg. 228)

"I am the Mind of God in eternity." (pg. 229)

"I am all there is in the illusion of all there is and is not." (pg. 229)

"All I am is all I love and all I can ever be. Love is my code, and allowing love in my heart is the key." (pg. 229)

"God Mind become my mind, and bend reality in my favor." (pg. 240)

"Fairies, heal my life-mind, allowing me to be healed in God Mind in nature." (pg. 247)

"Earth life, heal my lifetimes in God Mind, allowing all of my lifetimes to be an easy illumination of God Mind wisdom and God Mind peace, healed in the Mind of God as an Earth life healed." (pg. 250)

"All energy in my mind is loving energy." (pg. 261)

"All of my energy in the universe loves me." (pg. 261)

"Allow my loving all of life hologram to not be disturbed." (pg. 262)

"Activate love into all that my heart projects, making a hologram of loving intentions." (pg. 263)

"Healing is winning; I am the winner." (pg. 270)

"All I have won is in this cup of love and peacefulness, and my cup runneth over." (pg. 270)

"I love myself, and I love my healed thoughts—making me a healed projector of a healed universe." (pg. 271)

"All I have done, all I have defended, and all I have declared in my life, will be allowed to heal in my mind as a learning lesson that I love." (pg. 271)

"I love all that I am." (pg. 278)

"Loving 'all that I am' is all I can ever be, creating God Mind in 'all that I am'. All I am is God Mind, all I can ever be is God Mind, and God Mind is all there is. Will God Mind exclude 'all that I am' from all that there is? A separation is not possible, except in an illusion." (pg. 278)

"All heals in my mind, forgiving myself for all that I did and did not do—and all I could have done in the future, and it heals in God Mind now. All heals in God Mind in eternity." (pg. 315)

"I allow all that I hear, feel, and entertain inflammatory thoughts about—to heal in God Mind, the anti-inflammatory." (pg. 317)

"God Mind is my anti-inflammatory." (pg. 317)

Dismissing demons—"Demons, devils, and destructive thought forms—acclimate yourselves to God Mind allowed to heal in love, only flowing God Mind." (pg. 324)

Shielding from demons—"Demons, devils, and negative thought forms—all hatred heals in the light of God Mind coming from each of my cells. Nothing can diminish it." (pg. 325)

"I am God Mind." (pg. 327)

"God Mind is my universal projection, healing my mind and manifesting my desires." (pg. 328)

Affirm God Mind in the life-mind as hope, love, and wonder by asking yourself this question— "How can I love myself as God, hoping that God loves me, as I wonder how God could love itself as me?"

Answer acknowledging with another question— "Why not? God is all that I am, healing all that I am not—which is an illusion." (pg. 330)

Afterword

People have said to me that there must be more than 4 secrets of the universe.
All are included in the four main secrets, and in the design principle that is written in this book.

Good. I thought I may have to write more volumes, not that I mind writing more books.
You will compile a few more books about death, life, and healing in them.

Glossary

ONENESS: Infinity healed illuminating in God Mind.

GOD MIND: All twoness healed and illuminating in Oneness.

LIFE-MIND: Left-brain hemispheres healing and illuminating in an open portal in time.

LIGHT MIND: Right-brain hemispheres opening into the Mind of God.

LIGHT MIND OF GODNESS: Alternating healing and healed in life-mind allowing God Mind.

PORTAL: An opening in DNA, lighting open in God Mind.

FILAMENTS: Undulating light sensors, halting or allowing light into life through life's DNA.

ILLUMINATION: A healing light in your mind, or a healed light in God Mind.

LIGHT: All electrons and photons flowing into life.

MERKABAH: A light-activated God Mind illumination in the hologram of life, allowing itself a time and place illusion to heal in.

TIMELESSNESS: All healed in God Mind, not in the life-mind.

TIME: The lightness of being alternating in the life-mind as the illusion of moving in a progression.

NATURE: All of life healing in the Mind of God.

DEATH: Lighting open healed infinitely in Oneness.

INFINITY: All one instant in the Mind of God.

> "Keep the fires of love burning
> in your hearts day by day,
> for the love of God is manifested
> in the Earth through those
> that are just kind one to another."
>
> —Edgar Cayce

About the Author

From God Mind:

*Paul Gorman illuminates as a spiritual researcher,
writing his discoveries into books,
allowing healing in the minds
of all who read them.*

www.ingramcontent.com/pod-product-compliance
Lightning Source LLC
Chambersburg PA
CBHW030543080526
44585CB00012B/238